Small
Victories

Small Victories

Spotting Improbable

Moments of Grace

ANNE LAMOTT

RIVERHEAD BOOKS
a member of Penguin Group (USA)
New York
2014

RIVERHEAD BOOKS
Published by the Penguin Group
Penguin Group (USA) LLC
375 Hudson Street
New York, New York 10014

USA · Canada · UK · Ireland · Australia
New Zealand · India · South Africa · China

penguin.com
A Penguin Random House Company

Some of these essays have appeared, in slightly different
form and some under other titles, in *O: The Oprah Magazine*;
Salon; *Grace (Eventually): Thoughts on Faith*; *Plan B: Further
Thoughts on Faith*; and *Traveling Mercies: Some Thoughts on Faith*.

The author gratefully acknowledges permission to reprint "In the
Evening" by Billy Collins, from *The Trouble with Poetry and Other
Poems*, copyright © 2005 by Billy Collins. Reprinted by permission.

Library of Congress Cataloging-in-Publication Data

Lamott, Anne.
Small victories : spotting improbable moments of grace / Anne Lamott.
p.   cm.
ISBN 978-1-59448-629-6
1. Spiritual life.   2. Grace.   3. Hope.   4. Joy.   5. Life—Religious
aspects—Christianity.   6. Lamott, Anne—Religion.   7. Novelists,
American—20th century—Biography.   8. Christian biography—United
States.   I. Title.   II. Title: Spotting improbable moments of grace.
BL624.L352   2014   2014026967
248—dc23

Printed in the United States of America
3   5   7   9   10   8   6   4

BOOK DESIGN BY AMANDA DEWEY

To my guys, Sam, Jax, Stevo, John,
and Tyler Lamott, and Mason Reid.

Doomed without you.

Contents

The heads of roses begin to droop.
The bee who has been hauling his gold
all day finds a hexagon in which to rest.

In the sky, traces of clouds,
the last few darting birds,
watercolors on the horizon.

The white cat sits facing a wall.
The horse in the field is asleep on its feet.

I light a candle on the wood table.
I take another sip of wine.
I pick an onion and a knife.

And the past and the future?
Nothing but an only child with two different masks.

—Billy Collins, "In the Evening"

Small
Victories

Prelude:
Victory Lap

The worst possible thing you can do when you're down in the dumps, tweaking, vaporous with victimized self-righteousness, or bored, is to take a walk with dying friends. They will ruin everything for you.

First of all, friends like this may not even think of themselves as dying, although they clearly are, according to recent scans and gentle doctors' reports. But no, they see themselves as fully alive. They are living and doing as much as they can, as well as they can, for as long as they can.

They ruin your multitasking high, the bath of agitation, rumination, and judgment you wallow in, without the decency to come out and just say anything. They bust you by being grateful for the day, while you are obsessed with how thin your lashes have become and how wide your bottom.

My friend Barbara had already been living with Lou Gehrig's disease for two years on the spring morning of our Muir Woods hike. She had done and tried everything to stem the tide of deterioration, and you would think, upon seeing her with a fancy four-wheeled walker, needing an iPad-based computer voice named Kate to speak for her, that the disease was having its way. And this would be true, except that besides having ALS, Barbara had her breathtaking mind, a joyously bottomless thirst for nature, and Susie.

Susie, her girlfriend of thirty years, gave her an unfair advantage over the rest of us. We could all be great, if we had Susie. We could be heroes.

Barbara was the executive director of Breast Cancer Action, the bad girls of breast cancer, a grassroots advocacy group with a distinctly bad attitude toward the pink-ribbon approach. Susie was her ballast, and I had spoken at a number of their galas and fund-raisers over the years. Barbara and Susie were about the same height, with very short dark hair. They looked like your smartest cousins, with the beauty of friendly, intelligent engagement and good nature.

Barbara's face was set now, almost as a mask, like something the wind is blowing hard against, and she'd lost a lot of weight, so you could see the shape of her animal, and bones and branches and humanity. Yet she still had a smile that got you every time, not a flash of high-wattage white teeth, but the beauty of low-watt, the light that comes in through the bottom branches; sweet, peaceful, wry.

We set off. She was our lead duck, our cycling leader—the only person on wheels sussing up what lay before us at the trailhead, watching the path carefully because her life depended on it. Susie walked ever so slightly behind. I walked behind, in the slipstream.

Even on the path that leads through these woods, you feel the wildness. The trees are so huge that they shut you up. They are like mythical horse flanks and elephant skins—exuding such life and energy that their stillness makes you suspect they're playing Red Light, Green Light.

The three of us had lunch in town two months earlier, before the feeding tube, before Kate. Barbara used the walker, which looked like a tall, compact shopping cart, but moved at a normal pace. She still ate with a fork, not a feeding tube, and spoke, although so softly that sometimes I had to turn to Susie for translation. Barbara talked about her wellness blog, her need for supplemental nutrition. Breath, nutrition, voice; breath, nutrition, voice. (She posted a list on her blog from time to time, of all the things she could still do, most recently "enjoy the hummingbirds; sleep with my sweetie. Speak out for people with breast cancer.")

Now she is silent. When she wants to talk, she can type words on her iPad that Kate will then speak with efficient warmth. Or she can rest in silence. She knows that even this diminished function and doability will be taken one day at a time. When you are on the knife's edge—when nobody knows exactly what is going to happen next, only that it will be worse—you take in today. So here we were, at the trailhead, for a cold day's walk.

I'm a fast walker, because my dad had long legs and I learned to keep up, but today a walk with Barbara was like Mother May I? May I take a thousand baby steps? Barbara seemed by her look of concentration to align herself with all the particles here in the looming woods, so she could be as present and equal as possible. She couldn't bother with saying anything unimportant, because she had to type it first. This relieved all of us from making crazy chatter.

This is a musical grove. The redwoods are like organ pipes, playing silent chords. Susie pointed out birds she knew, and moved a few obstacles on our route, as Barbara rolled on. Susie is the ultimate support, a weight-bearing wall. She's not "I am doing wondrous things," but simply helping both herself and Barbara be comfortable in the duo of them. She has lots of sly humor, but no gossipy edge, except in a pinch.

I have been to Muir Woods hundreds of times in my life, from my earliest days. This was where my family brought visitors. I got lost here at four, amid the crowds, but it was different fifty years ago. For the parents, a missing child was scary, yet you did not assume the child was dead. I was always afraid, lost or not. I got lost so often—once for more than half an hour among sixteen thousand people at the Grand National Rodeo—that until I was seven, I had notes pinned to my coats, little cards of introduction, with my name and phone number: If found, please return, as if I were a briefcase. I have gotten lost all of my life, maybe more than most, and been found every time. Even though I believe that the soul is immortal and grace bats last, I'm afraid because Barbara is going to die, and Susie will be all alone.

I love Wendell Berry's lines that "it may be that when we no longer know what to do, we have come to our real work, and that when we no longer know which way to go, we have begun our real journey. The mind that is not baffled is not employed. The impeded stream is the one that sings."

I have a lot of faith and a lot of fear a lot of the time.

The day was so cold that for once Muir Woods did not smell of much; heat brings out stronger smells, but today was crisply delicious. We walked along the path like kids moving as slowly as one humanly can.

We rounded the first curve, *vrrrooom*. Susie and I spoke of nothing in particular. Barbara pointed to her ear, and we stopped to listen, to the tinkle of the creek, and all the voices of the water. There was the interplay of birdsong and people song and the creek's conversation, as if it had a tongue, saying, "Keep going, we'll all just keep on going. You can't stop me or anything else, anyway." Every sound is by definition a stop, which is how we can hear it.

We were walking in step with Barbara, as she held on to her conveyance, and I felt myself take on all the qualities that Barbara brought to the day, a fraught joy and awareness. There was a frozen music in the giant redwoods, like a didgeridoo. The trees looked like they were wearing skirts of burl and new growth. I asked Barbara and Susie, "When you flip the skirts up, what do you get?" Barbara pointed to the answer: a tree that had toppled over—roots covered with moss and what looked like mossy coral, very octopus-like. Some tree trunks had roots wrapped up and around them, like barber poles. Some trunks were knuckly and muscular in their skirts, with many knees, and some burl seats for anyone who needed to sit.

The trees looked congregational. As we walked beneath the looming green world, pushing out its burls and sprouts, I felt a moment's panic at the thought of Barbara's impending death, and maybe also my own. We are all going to die! That's just so awful. I didn't agree to this. How do we live in the face of this? Left foot, right foot, push the walker forward.

When my son was six or seven, and realized that he and I were not going to die at the exact same moment, he cried for a while, and then said that if he'd known this, he wouldn't have agreed to be born.

Barbara looked at me gently. We studied each other like trees. Her smile was never used to ingratiate herself. This is so rare.

The ferns looked almost as if they had sprung from an umbrella shaft—you could click it and cock it, and the spokes would burst forth or could be put away.

We picked up speed and barreled around the next corner, going one mile an hour: Susie mentioned that they had to get back to San Francisco for a meeting. The city seemed far away, on another planet, but not as far away as a meeting. We passed a great show of burl in a thick lumpy flow, as if it had been arrested in downward movement, like mud or lava. One burl looked exactly like a bear cub. Ferns and sometimes whole redwoods spring from burl. The ferns remind you of prehistory. Dinosaurs hide behind them. They are elegant, tough, and exuberant, like feathers in a woman's hat.

I asked Barbara, "Are you afraid very often?" She shrugged, smiled, stopped to type on her laptop, and hit Send. Kate spoke: "Not today."

The glossy bay trees are so flexible, unlike some people I could mention (i.e., me), with long horizontal ballet arms. They are light and sun seekers, and when you are in the forest of crazy giants, you might have to do some sudden wild-ass moves, darting through a small slant of space among the giants—"Oh, wham—sorry—coming through—sorry. Sorry."

We were nearly to the end of the trail. I've always loved to see the foreigners here in their high heels, speaking Russian, Italian, happy as birds. Maybe they have Saint Petersburg and the Sistine Chapel back home, but we have this cathedral. Who knows what tragedies these happy tourists left behind at home? Into every life crap will fall. Most of us do as well as possible, and some of it works okay, and we try to release that which doesn't and which is never going to. On the list of things she could still do, Barbara included: "Clip my nails with a very large nail clipper, hear songs in my head, enjoy a baseball game, if the Giants or Orioles are winning." Making so much of it work is the grace of it; and not being able to make it work is double grace. Grace squared. Their somehow grounded buoyancy is infectious, so much better than detached martyrdom, which is disgusting.

This is not what Barbara and Susie signed up for, not at all. Mistakes were made: Their plan was to spend as much time as they could at Yosemite, the theater, Mendocino, and helping people with breast cancer. But they are willing to redefine themselves, and life, and okayness. Redefinition is a nightmare—we think we've arrived, in our nice Pottery Barn boxes, and that this or that is true. Then something happens that totally sucks, and we are in a new box, and it is like changing into clothes that don't fit, that we hate. Yet the essence remains. Essence is malleable, fluid. Everything we lose is Buddhist truth—one more thing that you don't have to grab with your death grip, and protect from theft or decay. It's gone. We can mourn it, but we don't have to get down in the grave with it.

Barbara pointed out a bird so tiny that Susie and I didn't see it at first in the fallen branches and duff of the forest floor. It was the only thing moving besides us humans. All of a sudden we saw a tiny jumpy camouflaged creature, heard the teeny tinkly peep. We performed the obeisance of delight. It is so quiet here, as though the trees are sucking up so much sound that anything that can get through them has a crystalline quality.

A great bay arch across the dirt was our last stop on the way. It was in full curvy stretch, arched all the way over our path, reaching for sun and touching the ground on the other side. I wondered if it would snake along on top of the duff, always following the light. It is nobody's fool. Lithe and sinewy, the branch looked Asian: I guess we're all Pacific Rim on this bus. All of its leaves were gone, as if it had spent its time and life force in the arching. Barbara trundled along up to it, smiled, and made the exact arch with her hand—like, Here's the arch and I'm saluting it, standing beneath it, and now walking through.

Companions

The Book
of Welcome

There must have been a book—way down there in the slush pile of manuscripts—that somehow slipped out of the final draft of the Bible. That would have been the chapter that dealt with how we're supposed to recover from the criticism session in the Garden, and discover a sense that we're still welcome on the planet. There are moments in Scripture when we hear that God delights in people, and I am incredulous. But they are few and far between. Perhaps cooler heads determined that too much welcome would make sissies out of us all, and chose instead accounts of the ever popular slaughter, exile, and shame.

The welcome book would have taught us that power and signs of status can't save us, that welcome—both offering and receiving—is our source of safety. Various chapters and verses of this book would remind us that we are wanted and even occasionally delighted in, despite the unfortunate truth that we are greedy-grabby, self-referential, indulgent, overly judgmental, and often hysterical.

Somehow that book "went missing." Or when the editorial board of bishops pored over the canonical lists from Jerusalem and Alexandria, they arbitrarily nixed the book that states un-equivocally that you are wanted, even rejoiced in.

We have to write that book ourselves.

Where can we begin, in the face of clearly not having been cherished for who we are, by certain tall, anxiously shut-down people in our childhood homes, whom I will not name? How far back does the sense of provisional welcome go? I would start with my first memory.

I am three years old, at our family cabin in Bolinas, before the town becomes a countercul-ture artists' community. My grandparents paid two thousand dollars for a rustic one-room cottage that was several hundred yards from Duxbury Point, from which you could see a great expanse of ocean, the horizon, and the reef below.

My grandparents, who had traveled the world

in their work as Christian missionaries, had brought back eight or so Mexican sorcery masks made of wood, and they hung these on the cabin wall. Each one had devil eyes surrounded in white that glowed in the dark. The fangs did, too. I had already begun my work as a lifelong insomniac, and would stay up or wake in the glare of these eyes and teeth, terrified to the core. I remember that when my parents tried, grumpily, to comfort me in the middle of the night, I pointed to these masks as the source of my terror. They said re-assuring things, like "Oh, for Chrissakes, Annie. Those are just masks!" Strangely, this did not help me sleep. So I'd crawl over onto my older brother's side of the trundle bed and drift off. My presence would wake him up. He would push me back onto my side of the bed. I would come crawling back like green slime. He'd bulldoze me with his feet. I'd come back. Then he would begin to hit me. Anyone would have hit me, I realize now. Jesus would have hit me.

Sometimes I even woke screaming from these nightmares at the cabin. This further endeared me to everyone. I also had dreams back at home where the masks had found me, ten towns away, and one in which my mother turned around at the stove with a spatula in one hand, her *sanpaku* eyes glittering behind a *bruja* mask with hemp hair. But the masks stayed up. Why didn't my parents or my grandparents replace them with something that made me feel safe, like, say, framed Audubon duck paintings? I was still afraid at eight and nine, and still couldn't sleep. By then I had migraines, too, and felt freakish and forlorn.

The reality is that most of us lived our first decades feeling welcome only when certain conditions applied: we felt safe and embraced only when the parental units were getting along, when we were on our best behavior, doing well in school, not causing problems, and had as few needs as possible. If you needed more from them, best of luck.

It also doesn't help that the planet is not nearly as hospitable as one might have hoped.

In the beginning, there was implantation, which was either the best or the worst news, and then God or life did some voodoo knitting that created each of us. We came into the world one by one. The next thing we knew, we were at the dinner table with delusional and unhappy people, who drank, or should have drunk, and who simultaneously had issues with rigidity and no boundaries. These people seemed to go out of their way to make it clear that we were not the children they'd had in mind. You were thwarting their good intentions with your oddness and bad posture.

They liked to think their love was unconditional. That's nice. Sadly, though, the child who showed up at the table for meals was not the child the parents had set out to make. They seemed surprised all over again. They'd already forgotten from breakfast.

The parental units were simply duplicating what they'd learned when they were small. That's the system.

It wasn't that you got the occasional feeling that you were an alien or a chore to them. You just knew that attention had to be paid constantly to their moods, their mental health levels, their rising irritation, and the volume of beer consumed. Yes, there were many happy memories marbled in, too, of picnics, pets, beaches. But I will remind you now that inconsistency is how experimenters regularly drive lab rats over the edge.

Maybe they knew the child was on to them, could see through them, could see the truth, could see how cracked, unstable, and distant they were. We knew their most intimate smells and sounds and vulnerabilities, like tiny spies. The whole game in the fifties and early sixties was for no one to know who you really were. We children were witness to the total pretense of how our parents wanted the world to see them. We helped them maintain this image, because if anyone outside the family could see who they really were deep down, the whole system, the ship of your family, might sink. We held our breath to give the ship buoyancy. We were little air tanks.

They knew deep down they were manic-depressive crazy people, but they wanted others to see them as good family men and women, peaceful warriors, worker bees, and activists who were making the world safe for democracy. Their kids knew about their tempers and vices, but the kids were under the wizard's spell, and also under the constant threat of exile or hunger.

The silver lining to this is that since the world we came into is an alcoholic, sick, wounded, wounding place, we also ended up with an owner's manual for dealing with craziness. We knew how to keep secrets. Also, our parents came with siblings who adored us, because we were not theirs. They actually *got* me. When I'd come through the door, the expression on my uncles' and aunts' faces would be so happy. There she is! There's Annie.

Isn't she something? The way they looked across the table at me, with pleasure and wonder, taught me what love looked like.

Their love was dependable refuge during the life-threatening teenage years. No one on earth feels less welcomed and more deformed than teenagers. Drinking was essential to my feeling semi-okay. Until I discovered booze, I'd always felt that I was invisible to the beautiful people, while under observation by my parents, and teachers, and most horribly, myself. I was so loved by best friends, yet I was scared a lot of the time, of many people, of failure, of sexual things that I thought or did or wanted to do. I developed a lot of charm, humor, and smarts, so I could bat the demons away. But they always came back.

Teachers began to welcome me, almost like friends, because I was smart, funny, and desperate. They gave me a lot of encouragement when I most felt like a complete loser, and then they gave me the great books that held the key to life: All humans felt alone, damaged, deformed, alien, and toxic. Toxic Я Us. And all of the great writers drank, except for Kafka and Nietzsche, neither of whom you exactly wanted to be when you grew up.

College gave me passionate friends, some of

whom stayed close, along with a sense of both political and creative purpose, from which I have not veered. But at some point you had to leave; you tried to make a life. You know the rest. The eerie carousel ride of adulthood, the warped music, gaudy paint, the vertigo of triumphs and hidden dangers in grown-up life.

High performance always made everything better. An awful lot of busyness helped, too, but not nearly as much as alcohol or sex, preferably both.

Then, in my thirties, my system crashed. I got sober, because I had gone crazy. A few women in the community reached out to me. They recognized me as a frightened lush. I told them about my most vile behavior, and they said, "Me, too!" I told them about my crimes against the innocent, especially me. They said, "Ditto. Yay. Welcome." I couldn't seem to get them to reject me. It was a nightmare, and then my salvation.

It turns out that welcome is solidarity. We're glad you're here, and we're with you. This whole project called you being alive, you finding joy? Well, we're in on that.

I learned early in sobriety that there were two points of view about me—how my close friends saw me, and how I saw myself. I figured it was obvious that I was a fraud, and kind of disgusting. My friends thought I was irresistible, profoundly worthy of trust. I thought at first that one view must be wrong, and I made the most radical decision, for the time being, to believe my friends. I welcomed my lovable self back, with a small party, just the cat, me, and imaginary cups of tea, which I raised with an outstretched pinkie.

This welcoming toward myself took a big adjustment, a rebalancing of my soul. There had been so much energy thrown into performance, achievement, and disguise. I felt I had gotten a permission slip for the great field trip, to the heart of myself, in the protection of a few trusted friends.

Frankly, I was hoping to see more white cliffs and beaches, fewer swamps and shadows, but this was real life, the nature of things, full of both wonder and rot.

As soon as I was able, my friends encouraged me to go back to reclaim the devious, dark part of me. I invited her in: Pull up a chair at the table, hon. We're having soup tonight.

So our families were train wrecks; we've ruined the earth; kids die all the time. How do we understand that something welcoming remains, sometimes hidden, that we can still trust? When all seems lost, a few friends, the view, and random last-ditch moments of grace, like Liquid Wrench, will do. Otherwise, I don't know. We don't exactly solve this problem, or much of anything, although one can learn to make a perfect old-fashioned, or blinis.

I've discovered that offering welcome helps a lot, especially to the deeply unpleasant or weird. The offer heals you both. What works best is to target people in the community whom no one else seems to want. Voilà: now welcome exists in you.

We want you, as is. Can you believe it? Come on in. Sit down. Let me get you a nice cup of tea. Would you like a lime juice bar?

From the time I got sober and started remembering my dreams in the morning, the old cabin has been the setting for most of the dreams that involve my family. It is a stand-in for the dinner table, for the saga of intergenerational sickness, mental illness, secrecy. My very favorite dream featured a family reunion years ago, where my grown brothers had gathered for a meal at the dining table with our parents, who were alive and healthy. The cabin looked like it had been tricked out by Laura Ashley, with bed skirts on the trundle beds, doilies on the chairs. Sadly, though, someone had tracked in dog poop, and gotten it all over the rugs and bed skirts. My younger brother leaned over at the table to whisper in my ear, "This would be such a cozy place, if there wasn't shit all over everything."

That pretty much says it for me. I'm sure your family was fine, and if that is the case, never mind. But I have needed a book of welcome for such a long time. I didn't know how to let go of judging people so quickly, on how they look, or dress, or speak, so I couldn't stop judging myself. I didn't know welcome was a matter of life and death. Look how often lonely people kill themselves, or others. Look at what squandered and ridiculous lives most people lead.

Until recently I barely even knew the signs of welcome, like the way a person plopped down across from me and sighed deeply while looking at me with relief: a shy look on someone's face that gave me time to breathe and settle in. I didn't know that wounds and scars were what we find welcoming, because they are like ours.

Trappings and charm wear off, I've learned. The book of welcome says, Let people see you. They see that your upper arms are beautiful, soft and clean and warm, and then they will see this about their own, some of the time. It's called having friends, choosing each other, getting found, being fished out of the rubble. It blows you away, how this wonderful event happened—me in your life, you in mine.

Two parts fit together. This hadn't occurred all that often, but now that it does, it's the wildest experience. It could almost make a believer out of you. Of course, life will randomly go to hell every so often, too. Cold winds arrive and prick you; the rain falls down your neck; darkness comes. But now there are two of you. Holy Moly.

The book of welcome says, Don't blow it! The two nonnegotiable rules are that you must not wear patchouli oil—we'll still love you, but we won't want to sit with you—and that the only excuse for bringing your cell phone to the dinner table is if you're waiting to hear that they've procured an organ for your impending transplant.

At the age of sixty, I finally realized that I had been raised not to say "You're welcome," and I began to wonder how this habit had reinforced my sense of separation. When I grew up, girls were taught to minimize how much they had given, how much time and hard work something had taken.

It might not even be noticed at first, because people expected you to do things for them. They felt entitled to largesse. So there was a double abnegation—your possibly sacrificial act of generosity wasn't noticed the first four times, and then when you were finally thanked, you were taught to respond, "Don't mention it." Or, "You'd have done the same." Glad to do it. It's *nothing.*

If generosity is nothing, then what is anything?

Now I make myself accept gratitude. I look people in the eye, and say gently, "You're really welcome." I might touch their cheeks with the backs of my fingers. This simple habit has changed me.

For instance, this morning I dreamed I was in the cabin, boxing up things for a move. This very morning, God is my witness. I thought I was alone, but my younger brother kept showing up to help me with the move, taking furniture and books out to a borrowed truck. He drove me to my new cottage, near Agate Beach, where we spent our childhoods walking with our parents, looking for sea glass and fossilized bits of whale bone, peering into tide pools, sometimes falling in. The new cottage was warm and shabby chic, but each time we went back to the old cabin for another load, my heart ached with what a great little place it had been. After unloading the boxes of books from the truck, we climbed into my 1959 Volkswagen Bug and I drove us to a gathering of sober alcoholics in the old town library. There were the familiar worn hardwood floors, and candles and the lifelike plastic flowers you see on Buddhist altars. There was a man in the parking lot selling *eighteen* varieties of real yellow flowers from a flatbed truck. Then an ancient German woman, whose groceries I'd been carrying because she seemed frail, opened my VW by sharply wrenching the door handle, which had apparently been stuck. She said to me, "Oh, this sometimes happens to my cars, too. It will be fine for the time being. Thank you for your help."

I said, "You are quite welcome." And I awoke.

Ladders

In May 1992, I went to Ixtapa with my son, Sam, who was then two and a half. At the time, my best friend of twenty years, named Pammy, had been battling breast cancer for two years. I also had a boyfriend with whom I spoke two or three times a day, whom I loved and who loved me. Then, in early November of that year, the big eraser came down and got Pammy, and it also got the boyfriend, from whom I parted by mutual agreement. The grief was huge, monolithic.

All those years I fell for the great palace lie that grief should be gotten over as quickly and as privately as possible. But what I've discovered since is that the lifelong fear of grief keeps us in a barren, isolated place and that only grieving can heal grief;

the passage of time will lessen the acuteness, but time alone, without the direct experience of grief, will not heal it. San Francisco is a city in grief, we are a world in grief, and it is at once intolerable and a great opportunity. I'm pretty sure that only by experiencing that ocean of sadness in a naked and immediate way do we come to be healed—which is to say, we come to experience life with a real sense of presence and spaciousness and peace. I began to learn this when Sam and I returned to the same resort three months after Pammy's death.

I took him back partly for reasons of punctuation. He was different this time, though. We both were. I had discovered that I could just barely live without Pammy. Whenever I went to her house to visit her daughter, Rebecca, I heard Pammy's flute, remembered exactly the yellow of her hair, felt stalked by her absence, noted by it. It was like the hot yellow day that Faulkner describes in *Light in August* as "a prone and somnolent yellow cat," contemplating the narrator. At any moment, the cat might suddenly spring.

Also, I was a little angry with men at the time, and scared; in the aftermath of the romantic loss, my heart felt like it had a fence surrounding it. Now

Sam seemed to be standing with me behind this fence; he seemed to feel safe only around me. He was sweet and friendly but shyer, no longer the social butterfly he had been the year before, when Pammy had still been alive. Back then I could leave him all day in the resort's child-care program. This time he was clingy and heavily Oedipal. I began to call myself Jocasta; he began to call me darling.

The first year, I'd come here alone with Sam. I mostly swam and ate by myself, walking into the dining area three times a day feeling shy and odd, cringing, with my arms stiffly at my sides like Pee-wee Herman. But this year I was with my friend Tom, an extremely funny Jesuit and sober alcoholic, who drank like a rat for years and smoked a little non-habit-forming marijuana on a daily basis. He also did amyl nitrate, although he said that this was just to get to know people.

His best friend, Pat, was along, too. I found that I could hardly stand for people to have best friends who were still alive. But when Sam and I had breakfast with both of them at the airport the morning we left for Mexico, they made me laugh and forget myself.

Pat is a very pretty woman in her late forties who is about a hundred pounds overweight, and sober seven years.

"Pat has a lot of problems," Tom told us over breakfast.

"This is true," said Pat.

"She was sober for four years," he continued, "until her husband got brain cancer. Then for a few years she had a little social Tylenol with codeine every day, with the merest slug of NyQuil every night for a cold that just wouldn't go away."

"I was a little depressed," she said.

After breakfast, we flew to Ixtapa. Adobe haciendas, cobblestone paths, a long white beach, palm trees, bougainvillea, warm ocean water—and no one back home desperately hoping I'd call.

Grief, as I read somewhere once, is a lazy Susan. One day it is heavy and underwater, and the next day it spins and stops at loud and rageful, and the next day at wounded keening, and the next day at numbness, silence. I was hoarse for the first six weeks after Pammy died and my romance ended, from shouting in the car and crying, and I had blisters on the palm of one hand from hitting the bed with my tennis racket, bellowing in pain and anger. But on the first morning in Mexico, the lazy

Susan stopped at feelings of homesickness, like those I had when my parents sold the house where I grew up.

I woke before Sam and lay in my bed in the cool, white adobe room, filled with memories of my first day there the year before. I remembered calling Pammy and my lover that first morning, how they gasped with pleasure to hear my voice. I lay there thinking this time that I had made a dreadful mistake to return, that I was not ready to laugh or play or even relax, and I wondered whether God had yet another rabbit He or She could pull out of the hat. Then my Oedipal little son woke up and hopped over to my bed. He patted my face for a while and said tenderly, "You're a beautiful girl."

The year before, when I dropped him off at the thatched child-care unit, we'd walk holding hands, and on the way he'd cry out joyfully, "Hi, Sky, my name is Sam. I yike you," because he couldn't say his *l*'s. "Hi, Yeaf," he'd say happily to the leaves, "my name is Sam. I yike you." It seemed very long ago. This year he looked at me all the time like a mournful fiancé and said, "I want to kiss you on the *y*ips."

On the third day in Mexico, Tom told me that Jung said, sometime after his beloved wife died, "It cost me a great deal to regain my footing. Now I am free to become who I truly am." And this is God's own truth: The more often I cried in my room in Ixtapa and felt just generally wretched, the more often I started to have occasional moments of utter joy, of feeling aware of each moment shining for its own momentous sake. I am no longer convinced that you're supposed to get over the death of certain people, but little by little, pale and swollen around the eyes, I started to feel a sense of reception, that I was beginning to receive the fact of Pammy's death, the finality. I let it enter me.

I was terribly erratic, some moments feeling so holy and serene that I was sure I was going to end up dating the Dalai Lama. Then the grief and craziness would hit again, and I would be in Broken Mind, back in the howl.

The depth of the feeling continued to surprise and threaten me, but each time it hit again and I bore it, like a nicotine craving, I would discover that it hadn't washed me away. After a while it was like an inside shower, washing off some of the rust and calcification in my pipes. It was like giving a dry garden a good watering.

Don't get me wrong: grief sucks, it really does. Unfortunately, though, avoiding it robs us of life, of the now, of a sense of living spirit. Mostly I have tried to avoid it by staying very busy, working too hard, achieving as much as possible. You can often avoid the pain by trying to fix other people; shopping helps in a pinch, as does romantic obsession. Martyrdom can't be beat. While too much exercise works for many people, it doesn't for me, although I have found that a stack of magazines can be numbing and even mood-altering. The bad news is that whatever you use to keep the pain at bay robs you of the flecks and nuggets of gold that feeling grief will give you. A fixation can keep you nicely defined and give you the illusion that your life has not fallen apart. But since your life may indeed have fallen apart, the illusion won't hold up forever, and if you are lucky and brave, you will want to bear disillusion. You begin to cry and writhe and yell and then to keep on crying; and finally, grief ends up giving you the two best gifts: softness and illumination.

Every afternoon when I'd pick Sam up at the kids' club, it was as if he'd spent the day in a workshop on Surviving the Loss of Your Mother. When I'd appear Lazarus-like to take him back to our room, his joy was huge. We always stopped to watch the iguanas that gathered on the grass near the lagoon, the giant adults like something out of *Jurassic Park*, the babies from Dr. Seuss. They were so wonderfully absurd and antediluvian that it was like communion among you and them and something ancient.

We spent a lot of time in our room, too. It was air-conditioned. Sam, so solemn and watchful, frequently brought up the last time he had seen Pammy, on Halloween, three days before she died. He was dressed as a sea monster, and he sat on her bed and they sang "Frère Jacques" together. He went over and over the facts of the evening: "She was in her jammies?" "Yes." "I was in my sea monster costume?" "That's right."

I thought a lot about the effect of Pammy's death on Sam, my own stunned attempts with that, the worry he voiced every few days that if Rebecca's mother could die, then wasn't it possible that his could, too? I somehow felt that all I had to offer was my own willingness to feel bad. I figured that eventually the tectonic plates inside me would shift, and I would feel a lessening of the pain. Trying to fix him, or distract him, or jolly him out of his depression would actually be a disservice. I prayed for the willingness to let him feel sad and displaced until he was able to stop slogging through the confusion and step back into the river of ordinariness.

The sun beat down, the hours passed slowly to the drone of the air conditioner. I kept starting to cry and then falling asleep. Sometimes grief looks like narcolepsy.

One afternoon in our room I had been crying a little, while Sam dozed in his own bed. Then I fell deeply asleep. I woke much later to find Sam standing by my bed, tugging at my sleeve, looking at me earnestly with his huge googly extraterrestrial eyes. He cleared his throat and then said something I guess he must have heard on TV. He said, "Excuse me, mister."

It made my heart hurt. I thought I was going to die. In "Song of Myself," Whitman wrote, "To touch my person to some one else's is about as much as I can stand."

There was a man at the resort with a prosthetic leg. I'd seen it lying around by the pool a few times before I actually saw him, and when I did, he was climbing a trapeze ladder in the circus grounds. Circus school was held at the resort every afternoon at three, on the lawn between the haciendas and the beach, using an elaborate rig of ropes and swings and netting. The man, whose name turned out to be Steve, was wearing shorts, and his stump was visible an inch or two below the hemline—and I've got to say that this kicked the shit out of my feeling self-conscious in shorts because of my cellulite and stretch marks.

He climbed the ladder with disjointed grace, asymmetrical but not clumsy, rung by rung, focused and steady and slow. Then he reached the platform, put on his safety harness, and swung out over the safety net, his one leg hooked over the bar of the trapeze as he swung back and forth, finally letting go. A teacher on the other trapeze swung toward him, and they caught each other's hands and held on, and swung back and forth for a while. Then the man dropped on his back to the safety net and raised his fist in victory. "Yes!" he said, and lay there on the net for a long time, looking at the sky with a secret smile.

I approached him shyly at lunch the next day and said, "You were great on the trapeze. Are you going to do it again?" And I had this idea that he might, so that I could do some serious writing about spirit and guts and triumph. But all he said was, "Honey, I got much bigger mountains to climb."

Life does not seem to present itself to me for

my convenience, to box itself up nicely so I can write about it with wisdom and a point to make before putting it on a shelf somewhere. Now, at this stage of my life, I understand just enough about life to understand that I do not understand much of anything. You show me a man with one leg climb up a trapeze ladder, and the best I can do is to tell you that when I saw him, he was very focused and in a good mood.

The next day I saw his plastic leg lying on a beach towel at the far end of the beach, where the windsurfing lessons take place. Oh dear, I thought. The shoelace of the expensive sneaker on the foot of the plastic leg was untied. I went and tied it, and then sat down in the sand. I really wanted to ask how he'd lost his leg and how he got back on his feet, when one was now made of plastic. I remembered how, a few months before Pammy died, we read a line by the great Persian mystical poet Rumi: "Where there is ruin, there is hope for a treasure." Pammy and I talked at the time of a sunken ship on the bottom of the ocean, full of jewels and gold; it was there in the heightened sense of existence and of the sacred that we felt in the midst of the devastation of her illness. It was there in the incredible sense of immediacy and joy we had felt some days toward the end, cruising malls and parks, Pammy in her wheelchair, wearing a wig, lashing me with a blue silken scarf to go faster. I sat on the beach hoping to see the man again, thinking of how much we lose yet how much remains, but it was getting late and I needed to go pick up Sam, and I left before Steve returned.

My new friend Pat had gone snorkeling almost every afternoon and loved it more than any other activity, although because of her weight it was im-possible for her to climb back into the boat un-aided. On the day before we left Mexico, I decided to give it a try. The snorkel boat left at three in the afternoon and took a group of people to a cove twenty minutes across the bay. Over lunch, though, I started to chicken out, until Pat said I had to go, that we couldn't be friends if I didn't. "Then tell me what you love most about it," I said. She thought for a while, and a faraway, almost sensuous look came over her face. "I like picking out the guys who are going to help push my big, wet, slippery body back up the ladder onto the boat," she said slowly.

Tom and I ended up going together. The little cove was hidden around the corner from a beach with grass huts and umbrellas on the white sands; cactuses on the ancient neighboring hills framed it all. We donned our gear and jumped in. The water is not crystal clear, and there are not a million brilliantly colored fish to watch, but if there is a heaven—and I think there really may be one—it may be similar to snorkeling: dreamy, soft, bright, quiet.

At first my breath underwater sounded labored and congested, like the Keir Dullea character's in *2001: A Space Odyssey* when he's in the pod outside the mother ship. I floated off by myself. Then, in the silence, I felt for a while as if I were breathing along with everything in the world. It is such a nice break from real life not to have to weigh anything. Beautiful plants swayed in the current; funny little fish floated past.

I daydreamed about Pammy. Near the end she said of her young daughter, "All I have to do to get really depressed is to think about Rebecca, and all I have to do to get really joyful is to think about Rebecca." I floated around slowly, crying; the mask filled up with tears—I could have used a windshield wiper. I felt very lonely. I thought maybe I wouldn't feel so bad if I didn't have such big pieces of Pammy still inside me, but then I thought, I want those pieces in me for the rest of my life, whatever it costs me. So I floated along, still feeling lonely but now not quite so adrift. I starting thinking of Pat, big and fat and comfortable enough to wear a swimsuit in front of us. I laughed, remembering what she'd said about the ladder, and I accidentally swallowed water. I watched the small fish swim in and out of the feathery sea plants, and I thought of beautiful, wild, happy Rebecca. This made my heart hurt, too, yet I felt a little lighter inside. And just then Tom came paddling over, and I was aware of his presence beside me although I couldn't actually see his face, and for the longest time we lay there bobbing on the water's surface, facedown, lost in our own worlds, barely moving our fins, side by side.

Forgiven

I went around saying for a long time that I am
not one of those Christians who are heavily
into forgiveness—that I am one of the other
kind. But even though it was funny, and actually
true, it started to be too painful to stay this way.
They say we are punished not for the sin but by the
sin, and I began to feel punished by my unwilling-
ness to forgive. By the time I decided to become
one of the ones who are heavily into forgiveness, it
was like trying to become a marathon runner in
middle age; everything inside me either recoiled,
as from a hot flame, or laughed a little too hysterically. I tried to will myself into forgiving various
people who had harmed me directly or indirectly

over the years—four former Republican presidents, three relatives, two old boyfriends, and one teacher in a pear tree—it was "The Twelve Days of Christmas" meets *Taxi Driver*. But in the end I could only pretend that I had forgiven them. I decided I was starting off with my sights aimed too high. As C. S. Lewis says in *Mere Christianity*, "If we really want to learn how to forgive, perhaps we had better start with something easier than the Gestapo."

So I decided to put everyone I'd ever lived with, slept with, or been reviewed by on hold, and to start with someone I barely knew whom I had hated only for a while.

I'd had an enemy—an Enemy Lite—for some time, the parent of a child in Sam's first-grade class, although she was so warm and friendly that it might have astounded her to learn that we were enemies. But I, the self-appointed ethical consultant for the school, can tell you that it's true. Somewhere in the back of my mind I knew she was divorced and maybe lonely, but she also had mean eyes. In the first weeks of school she looked at me as if I were a Rastafarian draft-dodger type and then, over time, as if I were a dazed and confused alien space traveler. Now, I'll be the first to admit that I had a certain amount of trouble adjusting once Sam started first grade. I couldn't seem to get the hang of things; there was too much to remember, too much to do. But Sam's first-grade teacher was so kind and forgiving that I just didn't trouble my pretty head about schedules, homework, spelling lists, and other sundry unpleasantries. Nor was I able to help out in the classroom much. There were all these mothers who were always cooking holiday theme-park treats for the class; they always drove the kids—including mine—on their field trips, and they seemed to read all the papers the school sent home, which I think is actually a little show-offy. Also, it gave them an unfair advantage. They knew, for instance, from the first day that Wednesdays were minimum days, with school out half an hour earlier than usual, and they flaunted it, picking up their kids at just the right time, week after week.

I somehow managed to make it into October without figuring out this scheduling quirk.

Finally, one Wednesday, I stopped by Sam's classroom and found him—once again—drawing with his teacher. The teacher said gently, "Annie? Did you not know that school gets out half an hour early on Wednesdays?"

"Ah," I said.

"Didn't you get the papers the school mailed to you this summer?"

I racked my brain, and finally I did remember some papers coming in the mail from school.

And I remembered really meaning to read them.

Sam sat there drawing with a grim, distant stare.

Well, my enemy found out.

She showed up two days later all bundled up in a down jacket, because it was cold and she was one of the parents who was driving the kids on a field trip. Now, this was not a crime against nature or me in and of itself. The crime was that below the down jacket she was wearing spandex bicycle shorts. She wears bicycle shorts nearly every day, and I will tell you why: because she can. She weighs about eighty pounds. She has gone to the gym almost every day since her divorce, and she does not have an ounce of fat on her body. I completely hate that in a person. I consider it an act of aggression against the rest of us mothers, who forgot to start working out after we had our kids.

Oh, and one more thing: She still had a Ronald Reagan bumper sticker on her white Volvo, seven years after he left the White House.

The day of the field trip she said sweetly, "I just want you to know, Annie, that if you have any other questions about how the classroom works, I'd really love to be there for you."

I smiled back at her. I thought such awful thoughts that I cannot even say them out loud because they would make Jesus want to drink gin straight out of the cat dish.

It drove me to my knees. I prayed about it. I prayed because my son loves her son, and my son is so kind that it makes me want to be a better person, a person who does not hate someone just because she wears spandex bicycle shorts. I prayed for a miracle; I wrote her name down on a slip of paper, folded it up, and put it in the box that I use as God's in-box. "Help," I said to God.

There wasn't much noticeable progress for a while. I was asked to bake something for the farewell party on the last day of school. I couldn't do it. I was behind in my work. Also, I was in a bad mood. But I at least went to the party, and I ate the delicious cookies my enemy made, and we mingled a little, and I thought that this was progress. Then she had to go and wreck everything by asking, "Did you bake anything?"

I don't bake. I baked for school once and it was

a bad experience. Sam was in kindergarten at the little Christian school he attended, and I baked a dozen cupcakes for his class Christmas party and set them out to cool. Sam and I went outside to sweep the AstroTurf. (Okay, okay, I also don't garden.) Suddenly Sadie came tearing outside—our dog, who was so obedient and eager to please. But there was icing in the fur of her muzzle and a profoundly concerned look on her face. Oh my God, she seemed to be saying with her eyes: Terrible news from the kitchen!

Sam looked at me with total disgust, like "You ignorant slut—you left the cupcakes out where the dog could get them."

The next morning I bought cupcakes at Safeway. Like I said: I don't bake.

I also don't push Sam to read. There wasn't much pressure for anyone to read in first grade, which was good because my kid was not reading. I mean, per se.

My enemy's child was reading proficiently, like a little John Kenneth Galbraith in a Spider-Man T-shirt. He is what is referred to as an "early reader." Sam is a "late reader." (Albert Einstein was a "late reader." Theodore Kaczynski was an "early

reader." Not that I am at all defensive on the sub-
ject. *Pas du tout.*)

Sam and this woman's child were in the
same second-grade class, too, and the next thing
I knew, she had taken a special interest in Sam's
reading.

She began the year by slipping me early first-
grade books that she thought maybe Sam could
read. And Sam could certainly read some of the
words in these books. But I resented her giving
them to us with a patronizing smile, as if to say her
child would not be needing them because he was
reading the new Joan Didion.

I went to the God box. I got out the piece of
paper with her name on it. I added an exclamation
point. I put the paper back.

One day not long after, she sidled up to me at
school and asked me if I had an extra copy of the
book I had written about being a mother. It is
black-humored and quite slanted: George H. W.
Bush was president when Sam was born, and
perhaps I was a little angry. I had these tiny opinions. I wrote an anti–George Herbert Walker Bush
baby book.

So when she asked for a copy, I tried to stall; I

tried to interest her in my anti-Reagan writing book. But she insisted.

A few days later, filled with a certain low-grade sense of impending doom, I gave her a copy, signed, "With all good wishes."

For the next few days, she smiled obliquely whenever I saw her at school, and I grew increasingly anxious. Then one day she came up to me in the market. "I read your book," she said, and winked. "Maybe," she whispered, because my son was only a few feet away, "maybe it's a good thing he doesn't read."

I wish I could report that I had the perfect comeback, something so polite and brilliantly cutting that Dorothy Parker, overhearing it in heaven, raised her fist in victory. But I could only gape at my enemy, stunned. She smiled very nicely and walked away.

I called half a dozen people when I got home and told them about how she had trashed me. And then I trashed her. And it was good.

The next time I saw her, she smiled. I sneered, just a little. I felt disgust, but I also felt disgusting. I got out my note to God. I said: Look, hon. I think we need bigger guns.

Nothing happened. No burning bush, no cereal

flakes dropping from heaven forming letters of instruction in the snow. It's just that God began to act like Sam-I-Am from *Green Eggs and Ham.* Everywhere I went there were helpful household hints on loving one's enemies, on turning the other cheek, and on how doing that makes you look in a whole new direction. There were admonitions about the self-destructiveness of not forgiving people, and reminders that this usually doesn't hurt other people so much as it hurts you. In fact, not forgiving is like drinking rat poison and then waiting for the rat to die. Suggestive fortune cookies, postcards, bumper stickers began to pop up here and there—everything but skywriting—yet I kept feeling that I could not, would not, forgive her in a box, could not, would not, forgive her with a fox, not on a train, not in the rain.

One Sunday when I was struggling with this, the Scripture reading came from the sixth chapter of Luke: "Forgive, and ye shall be forgiven." Now, try as I might, I cannot find a loophole in that. It does not say, "Forgive everyone, unless they've said something rude about your child." And it doesn't even say, "Just try." It says, If you want to be forgiven, if you want to experience that kind of love, you have to forgive everyone in your life—

everyone, even the very worst boyfriend you ever had—even, for God's sake, yourself.

A few days later I was picking Sam up at the house of another friend and noticed a yellowed clipping taped to the refrigerator with "FORGIVE-NESS" written at the top—as though God had decided to abandon all efforts at subtlety and just plain noodge. The clipping said forgiveness meant that God is for giving, and that we are here for giving, too, and that to withhold love or blessings is to be completely delusional. No one knew who had written it. I copied it down and taped it to my refrigerator. Then an old friend from Texas left a message on my answering machine that said, "Don't forget, God loves us exactly the way we are, and God loves us too much to let us stay like this."

Only, I think she must have misquoted it, be-cause she said, "God loves you too much to let you stay like this."

I looked nervously over both shoulders.

A couple of days later my enemy's boy came to play at our house, and then she came to pick him up just before dinner. And for the first time, while he gathered his things, she sat down on the couch, as if she had done this before, as if it were the most natural thing. I felt around inside my heart, and it was not so cold or hard. In fact, I even almost offered her a cup of tea because she seemed sad or maybe tired. I felt a stab of kindness inside, until her son came bounding out of Sam's room, shouting that he'd gotten 100 percent on his arithmetic test and Sam had gotten two wrong.

"Traitor!" Sam shouted from his room, and slammed the door.

By bedtime, Sam said he forgave the boy but didn't want to be friends anymore. I said he didn't have to be friends, but he did have to be kind. At breakfast, Sam said he still forgave him, but when we got to school he said that it had been easier to forgive him when we were farther away.

Still, several days later, when the mother called and invited him to come play that afternoon, Sam desperately wanted to go. She picked him up after school. When I went over to get him, she offered me a cup of tea. I said no, I couldn't stay. I was in my fattest pants; she wore her bicycle shorts. The smell of something baking, sweet and yeasty, filled the house. Sam couldn't find his knapsack, so I looked around for it. The surfaces of her house were covered with fine and expensive things.

"Please let me make you a cup of tea," she said again, and I started to say no, but this thing inside me used my voice to say, "Well . . . okay." It was awkward. In the living room, I silently dared her to bring up school, math tests, or field trips; I dared her to bring up exercise or politics. As it was, we had very little to talk about—I was having to work hard making sure she didn't bring up much of anything, because she was so goddamn competitive—and I sat there politely sipping my lemongrass tea. Everywhere you looked was more façade, more expensive stuff—show-offy I-have-more-money-than-you stuff, plus you're-out-of-shape stuff. Then our boys appeared, and I got up to go. Sam's shoes were on the mat by the front door, next to his friend's, and I went over to help him put them on. As I loosened the laces on one shoe, without realizing what I was doing, I snuck a look into the other boy's sneaker—to see what size shoe he wore. To see how my kid lined up in shoe size.

And I finally got it.

The veil dropped. I got that I am as mad as a hatter. I saw that I was the one worried that my child wasn't doing well enough in school. That I was the one who thought I was out of shape. And that I was trying to get her to carry all this for me because it hurt too much to carry it myself.

I wanted to kiss her on both cheeks, apologize for all the self-contempt I'd been spewing out into the world, all the bad juju I'd been putting on her by thinking she was the one doing harm. I felt like J. Edgar Hoover, peeking into the shoes of his nephew's seven-year-old friend to see how the Hoover feet measured up, idly wondering how the kid's parents would like to have a bug on their phone. This was me. She was the one pouring me more tea, she was the one who'd been taking care of my son. She was the one who seemed to have already forgiven me for writing a book in which I trashed her political beliefs; like God and certain parents do, forgiven me almost before I'd even done anything that I needed to be forgiven for. It's like the faucets are already flowing before you even hold out your cup to be filled. Before forgiveness.

I felt so happy there in her living room that I got drunk on her tea. I read once in a magazine that in Czechoslovakia, they say an echo in the woods always returns your own call, and so I started speaking sweetly to everyone—to the mother, to the boys. And my sweet voice started getting all over me, like sunlight, like the smell of the Danish baking in the oven, two of which she put on a paper plate and covered with tinfoil for me and Sam to take home. Now obviously, the woman has a little baking disorder. And I am glad.

Trail Ducks

At the height of summer, my least favorite season, one I would have skipped if I were God, one of my best friends had a breakdown. He is my age and almost like a brother to me, highly accomplished, well employed, newly married to a fabulous woman, and prone to severe depression. He had not been able to stop thinking about killing himself, even though he adores his wife, his son, his work, and us, his friends. So he had been in what he referred to as "the bin" for three weeks, and was now at a halfway house, where he would stay for two weeks before reentry into his life. I had not seen him in a few days, and one sultry evening, empty and anxious, I suddenly got it in my head to go visit him. It was five o'clock, three hours before visiting hours ended, and it made perfect sense that even in my mental and sweaty condition I would drive on the freeway for an hour to support him in dealing with the mess of his breakdown and rehab, the strain it put on his marriage, fatherhood, career. Maybe, subconsciously, it was to make myself feel holy and purposeful, and to buoy myself up.

Also, it would help me deal with my own loneliness, because I was going to drag someone else along with me. I knew just the person.

My friend Janine would agree to come, spur of the moment. She loves this man, too. She loves any excuse to escape from her house, where there were three kids, one of whom was recovering from a bleed in his brain, caused by tumor, along with the in-laws who had arrived to help her care for the kids. Now, you would think a woman with a sick kid would be exempt from being sucked into my good-idea field trips, but no, this is not how it works: see, it would help her, too. Two birds with one stone: Annie would be helping everyone! Plus, Janine would drive. She has a huge mega-car with GPS, a built-in hands-free speaker phone, a great stereo.

I printed out a map and directions from MapQuest before I went to her house. I brought two ice-cold bottles of water and a baggie full of almonds, which I believe have medicinal powers, like SSRIs and blueberries.

I drove to her house, which was bustling with good cheer. The kid who had been so sick sat watching TV, surrounded by loud love. I hugged all the teenagers and in-laws, and spent a few special quality Annie minutes with the recovering boy, cajoling him into a little chat. Then Janine and I set out for the town of Rohnert Park, which less chari-table people called Rodent Park, a mysterious place with lots of meth labs and trailer parks, to which I have rarely been. We felt very superior and orga-nized, in her perfect car, with our map, directions, water, and almonds. And we love each other's com-pany. We were both sober, crabby Christians, with a purpose: to bring our best selves to this dear friend, whose wife and child were at home while he recovered from suicidal fixation. Our directions gave us the confidence to start out on the journey, to get on the freeway and drive to the residential care facility, an hour away, one exit and two right turns off the freeway. Easy.

We didn't even turn on the GPS.

The sun seemed to be thinking about setting, and hung low in the sky, and it was lovely to be together, cruising along, talking about her son's slow but steady progress and our dear friend's sudden breakdown.

"It's all so lifey," Janine said. "It's why we love TV so much."

We drove for nearly an hour and then started watching for our exit. The car phone rang, and Janine took it without seeming to move a thing. Maybe she has an AT&T chip embedded behind her ear. At any rate, she said, "Hello?" and it turned out to be Cathy, the woman in charge of transporting Janine's car back from the hospital in Houston where her fourteen-year-old son had been in rehab. The car was going to be delivered the next day, and Janine made arrangements, which is to say, we both listened while the woman chattered. "Yes," Janine said a number of times. "The post office in town, at noon." I smiled and made the universal sign of chattering fingers. "Yes," she said again. "Noon. Yes, correct: the post office."

I studied the directions. But when Janine clicked off the phone, we noticed that none of the exits was listed, and we realized we had gone too far. So we pulled over and turned on Janine's GPS, shaking our heads and laughing at ourselves about what confident little schoolgirls we had been, gripping our MapQuest directions but not paying attention.

The GPS lady told us to make a U-turn and get back on the freeway, heading south. We had driven 11.2 miles too far. Eleven miles too far! Oh, well, we said, and drove south. We drove along, gossiping, eating toasted almonds, and were within two miles of our destination when Janine's wonderful husband, Alan, called from Europe. His name and cell phone number appeared on the GPS screen, replacing the map. His big booming voice came through the speakers, asking her if she had a few minutes, but she explained that we were nearly at our destination, and had already missed our exit once. Could she call him back as soon as we arrived?

All the pieces of the puzzle of Janine's impossible life and sick child had kind-of-sort-of come back together today, and she didn't want to bum anyone out, especially her husband, who'd been through so much. But there was a long, bad silence from his end. It was clear that he was in a state, not just out of the country. And not just in any country, but in Germany.

"Fine," he said. "Good NIGHT." She tried to wheedle him into a better mood and said she'd return his call within five minutes—but he'd hung up. Oh, well, we said again, shrugging. It seemed to be our mantra. It's actually not a bad prayer, either.

One mile away now by the map on the GPS, we went back to concentrating like children. We were going to get there with close to an hour left. The GPS lady said our exit was in .3 miles.

And right then, *Ring Ring Ring.*

Cathy's phone number replaced the map on the GPS screen. The Houston car-transport person had one more question.

We both laughed, even though I realized somehow that we were going to miss the turnoff again. There were construction signs everywhere down here, blocking our view of the exits. Janine took the call.

Cathy wanted to verify that there was only one post office in town.

Janine said, "Correct," and then covered her mouth. Now we were in hysterics, the kind women friends dissolve into where there is seriously risk of pee. I saw out of the corner of my eye that we were about to pass the exit. I yelped, and Janine hit the brakes, but she had to drive on or risk being hit by the car behind us.

We shook our heads and looked to the GPS for rerouting information, and it was then I understood that beneath the hysterics were the other kind, of weeping and gnashing of teeth. We drove another mile looking for an exit, but it was all wreckage and detour signs. What seems true is that something in life, on the highways or in our hearts, is *always* being installed, or being repaired, or being torn down for the next installation. Or the mess of the repair or tear-down is being cleaned up and cleared out. I wiped at my eyes, kind of confused about the tears, and wondered if Janine's massive car had a gift shop where I could buy some Kleenex. I found some in the glove box.

Somehow, now silenced, we took the overpass that got us back on 101 North, and we made a right turn, and then one more turn, and another, until we pulled up in front of our friend's halfway house. *Bzzzztt*, my BlackBerry buzzed with a text: Our friend's wife wanted me to know she appreciated our visiting her husband, but her feelings were hurt that we hadn't included her. She would have loved to be part of our outing.

I wrote back from the passenger seat that I loved her and was sorry but it had been spur-of-the-moment and I had rushed out the door without thinking.

Janine stayed in the car and called her husband in Germany. I could tell it was going to be an unhappy conversation. I got out and walked to the front door. I automatically became the take-charge auntie you'd think *anyone* would like to have step into their screwed-up life now: organized, positive, on board.

It was twenty past seven, which meant we still had forty minutes to visit. My friend was waiting near the door, expressing worry that something had happened to us, and he looked so vulnerable there—I felt terrible that we were late, and I hate when people are late, even for dinner or a movie, much less a situation like this—that I started to cry.

Tears just burst into my eyes, pooled, and ran down my cheeks. Of course I know by this late in life that laughter and weeping are connected at the hip, but I had so wanted to bring my friend the peace of God, and for life and comfort to work, however briefly. Is that so much to ask?

Yeah, well, good luck.

My friend showed me around. He had his own room, with a photo of his family, and books. It was sweet. I breathed into that fact, this hilarious demonstration of what you set as the direct trajectory of your goal and, instead, of how things tend to turn out in real life—the overshooting of exits, and Cathy, and the angry husband and the hurt wife, and the messes of our lives pulling on our hems like sticky two-year-olds—and how at the same time, you got where you wanted to be.

We sat on his bed in his small room for a moment, until Janine came through the doorway, shaking her head with exasperation at whatever she and her husband had talked about. Now she looked drawn and pale, like the mother of a kid with a brain tumor. She and our friend hugged. Everything suddenly felt awkward, and as if there was not nearly enough time. Here is the one tiny problem with good intentions: There are always uninvited voices and obstructions, nattering and nipping and whining and tugging at you. Always. The kernel, the motive, may be lovely, compassion and selflessness, wanting to be of service, and it is still nourishing, but there is the rest of the shit that comes with it. All of it takes so much more energy, and detours, to get anywhere in life, even to Rodent Park.

Janine's husband had only wanted comfort. Our friend's wife just wanted to be included, to have company and camaraderie in the hardship. Cathy at the car company wanted to make plans to return Janine's car, and to celebrate the completion of the toughest, saddest possible circuit—the family and the car back home after such a haul. Kind of a miracle, really.

Getting found almost always means being lost for a while.

The circuitous routes and endless interruptions continued inside the halfway house, with lost souls wandering around or sitting dazed in front of bad TV in the living room; two people sat in the den, where our friend had planned for us to sit and talk. *Here I wanted to bring my goddamn solace, and all the visiting solace rooms were taken!* It so sucked.

Our friend took us to the kitchen, where a number of people sat around the big table, strange and sad-looking. A hugely obese woman with a neck tattoo sat beside an emaciated man with glazed eyes. Talk about lifey. There was no room at the table for three more.

Disappointment crossed our friend's face, and he sighed, but we assured him it didn't matter, so we got plastic tumblers of cold water, and he led us next to a small library. There were more strange people sitting in the chairs here, too, as well as a nerdy young man with a scraped-up face who was hugging himself tightly, ignoring the visitors.

Then, as is almost always the case, God sent along a minder, who had noticed our distressed milling. It would have been hard not to: we looked like exhausted moose. She had come by to give the person in charge at the front desk a ride home when her shift was over. She seemed to understand that all we needed was to be together for a while. She said, "I have an idea. I personally love to hang out in the garage. It's hidden away and relaxed."

And the three of us found ourselves in the quiet, dim garage, with lamps, coffee tables, and floor fans jammed in everywhere, and boxes, shelves of books, bicycle helmets. It was like a hoarder's rec room. Our minder turned on a standing lamp for us. A minder and some light. Voilà— heaven.

We each got our own couch, shoved close together, and did the plop-and-flop in lovely familiarity. Now it seemed funny that we had gotten so lost, even with a map, GPS, directions . . . Sort of like real life.

And we got our brief reprieve. I thanked God for that tiny breath of peace. Who knows, maybe there would be another. You don't know what shape, and what crazy interruptions, it will take to experience it. But our faces were lit now with affection and amazement at the perfect solution in such humble and homely surroundings.

The garage gave us a taste of normality, which none of us had felt for a while because of all the grief and strangeness. You have to be grateful whenever you get to someplace safe and okay, even if it turns out it wasn't quite where you were heading. The light you see when people are in the tunnel of deep trouble is domestic flashes of recognition and kitchen comforts, not Blake's radiance, which would be my preference.

The sky had shifted again when we stepped outside to the dusk. There were hints of the dying sunset. The three of us stood at the open door, admiring the sky. When you're in the dark, you have to try to remember that it's a dance—dark, light, dark, light, dim. Or when you're in the sun but the clouds come, of course you instantly think,

Oh, God, now it's going to get cold and wet, and it's all fucked, but then you might remember that when it was dark an earlier time, your friends shined a little thin light on it, and you remember one thing that sort of helped, one more step you can take, maybe one more thing you can try. I was reminded of something my friend Tasha told me once, that when she and her friends hike in a group, they leave trail ducks for the stragglers, piles of rocks by the path to show that they've gone left here, or right. I had to laugh, standing there in the open door: If a map, directions, GPS, and numerous highway signs hadn't helped, would we have even noticed a duck made of rocks? Well, yeah: I think so, deep inside. We had gotten here tonight, with enough time, and there had been warmth and tumblers of cool water. The rocks that marked our path had been the desire in our hearts to be there for one another. Through the window next to where we stood in the doorway, hugging our friend good-bye, we could see our mindful minder putting on her jacket and the person who'd been in charge showing her notes to the man about to take the next shift.

'Joice to the World

My pastor, Veronica, said yesterday that God constantly tells us to rejoice, but to do that, to get our 'joice back, we need to have had joy before. And it's never been needed as badly as now, when the world is hurting so badly, because joy is medicine.

San Quentin may not seem the obvious place to go searching for joy, but my friend Neshama and I went there last week to teach inmates how to tell stories. I would work with them on the craft of writing, while Neshama, who found her voice through the oral tradition, would pass along what she's learned in her work at a guild where people teach one another to tell crafted stories from the stage.

I was glad to be there, for a number of reasons. First of all, because Jesus said that whatever you did to the least of His people, you did to Him, and the lifers in penitentiaries are the leastest people in this country. Just look to see whose budgets are being cut these days—the old, the crazies, the children in Head Start—and that's where Jesus will be. He also promised that God forgives the unlovable and the unforgivable, which means most of us—the lifers, me, maybe you.

Second, my father had taught English and writing at San Quentin during the 1950s and 1960s. He published stories in *The New Yorker* about his students, and then wrote a biography of San Quentin; I grew up hearing and reading about his students and the place itself. He did not bog down in complex moral and ethical matters— victims' rights, recidivism. He just taught the prisoners to read good books, to speak good English, and to write. My father treated them with respect and kindness, his main philosophical and spiritual position being: Don't be an asshole. My brothers and I stood outside the gates of San Quentin with him and his friends over the years, in protest and silent witness whenever someone was going to be gassed.

And last, I was happy to be there because one of the inmates, Wolf, the head of the Vietnam vets' group there, had asked me to help some of his friends with their writing.

I had been inside the grounds for worship services at night but had never visited during the day. When we went, it was pouring rain. Waiting outside the walls with Neshama, two San Quentin English teachers, and a friend from church, I felt aware of the violence and fear of the world. I hardly know what to feel most days, except grief and bug-eyed paranoia. But my faith tells me that God has skills, ploys, and grace adequate to bring light into the present darkness, into families, prisons, governments.

San Quentin is on a beautiful piece of land in Marin County, on the western shore of San Francisco Bay, with lots of sun, views of the bridges, hills, windsurfers. I tried not to worry as we waited. On Sundays, Veronica kept repeating what Paul and Jesus always said: Don't worry! Don't be so anxious. In dark times, give off light. Care for the least of God's people. She quoted the Reverend James Forbes as saying, "Nobody gets into heaven without a letter of reference from the poor." Obviously, "the poor" includes prisoners.

Jesus had an affinity for prisoners. He had been one, after all. He must have often felt anxiety and isolation in jail, but He identified with the prisoners. He made a point of befriending the worst and most hated, because His message was that no one was beyond the reach of divine love, despite society's way of stating the opposite. God, what a nut.

Finally, we stood outside an inner gate, showed our IDs to the guards, and got our hands stamped with fluorescent ink. "You don't glow, you don't go," said one cheerful, pockmarked guard, which was the best spiritual advice I'd had in a long time.

As we stepped into a holding pen, my mind spun with worries about being taken hostage, having a shotgun strapped to my head with duct tape. I don't think Jesus would have been thinking these same thoughts: everything in Him reached out with love and mercy and redemption. He taught that God is able to bring life from even the most death-dealing of circumstances, no matter where the terror alert level stands.

Our group was allowed to view the outer walls of the prison, which was opened in 1852. San Quentin possesses great European beauty— ancient-looking walls, elegant gun towers. It's like a set from Edgar Allan Poe. Someone with the right attitude could do something really nice with this place, something festive. It could be a cute bed-and-breakfast, say. Or a brewery. I did not know who would be inside, only that most of the convicts were murderers serving life sentences. I imagined that some would be sullen and shifty-eyed, and others charming cons, trying to win me over so I would marry them and get them better lawyers, and consort with them on alternate Tuesdays. I knew there'd be camaraderie, violence, and re-demption inside, because I'd read my father's ac-counts and the accounts of others. But those were written years ago, when you could still believe in caring for prisoners without being accused of being soft on crime.

Jesus was soft on crime. He'd never have been elected anything.

In the courtyard, we were met by several staff people, and then by Wolf and two of his friends, all polite and clean-shaven, with Vietnam vets caps on. We stood within the circle of prison buildings, in the center of concrete cell blocks. The grounds are brightly landscaped by the inmates, but the buildings look like a child's play structure that has been left outside for a hundred years—a plastic and castley hodgepodge of stone and concrete, ornate, crumbly, deteriorated.

There's razor wire everywhere, and a constant clanging and banging of gates and cells and doors. Guards carry arms and keys that could be from the Middle Ages. Prisoners walk all over the grounds, as slowly as monks, with nowhere much to go. Of course, we saw your better inmates, the really polite ones, not the hard cases, not the men on death row. Those we saw and spent time with seemed to be sliding by, relatively seamless and calm. They're mostly older; you sense that their testosterone levels are down.

I like that in a prisoner.

Wolf and his friends showed us classrooms, the chapel, and the hobby shop, where inmates work making wooden cable-car jewelry boxes and stained-glass hummingbirds and crosses. "Should you guys be trusted with knives and saws and extremely sharp implements?" I asked nicely.

They laughed. "We earned the privilege by good behavior," Wolf told me. He showed us the old dining hall with the long walls covered in murals done in black and brown shoe polish by inmates. The murals depicted California's history and their

own—the Miwok on Mount Tamalpais, Sir Francis
Drake on the beaches of West Marin, the Spanish
missions, the Gold Rush, heroes of labor, farm-
workers, artists, prisoners, saints—and hidden inside the pictures were secrets only the prisoners
could see.

We walked to the main cell block. The prison is
overcrowded. The prisoners are double-celled,
double-bunked. The cells are grotesque, like a
Croatian zoo. I understand how the families of
victims might think the prisoners deserve this,
but seeing them stuffed in these cages affected
me the same way seeing photos of the displayed
corpses of Saddam Hussein's sons did. You had
to ask yourself: Who are we? And what next?
Bloody heads on stakes outside the White House?

"What are you reading?" I asked a man in
one cell.

He held out his book: true crime by Ann Rule.

Wolf led us to another dining hall, where sixty
prisoners had gathered in bolted-down chairs near
a stage to hear us speak. Behind them, kitchen staff
and prisoners were preparing the next meal, with
guards nearby.

What you might call the aesthetics left something to be desired—an echoey, cavernous space,

like a hangar, metallic, with the racket of people preparing food. It smelled like cheap meat and old oil and white bread.

I went onstage, took a long, deep breath, and wondered, as usual, where to start. I told the prisoners the same things I tell people at writing conferences: Pay attention, take notes, give yourself short assignments, let yourself write shitty first drafts, ask people for help, and you own what happens to you. They listened dutifully.

Then I introduced Neshama, with a concern that the prisoners wouldn't quite get her—this intense grandmother with a nice big butt and fuzzy gray hair, wearing a loud plaid flannel dress. I had invited her because I love her stories and knew it would be more fun for me, and because some people at San Quentin, like Neshama, hate to write but love to read and tell stories.

I had extremely low expectations: I hoped a few prisoners might form a guild, like the one to which Neshama belongs; I hoped they wouldn't hurt her, or overcome her, or try to make her marry them. She walked to the mike and told her first story, her version of a folktale. It was about a man with no luck, who comes upon safety, wealth, and a beautiful woman, but is too busy looking for fancier luck, somewhere else, to even notice her. Neshama painted the story with her hands, leaning into the crowd, and drawing back, hopeful or aghast at the unlucky man's journey, smiling gleefully at the story's close. And the place went nuts. She stole the show right out from under me, like a rock star, while I looked as prim and mainstream as Laura Bush. Here they had thought Neshama was going to teach them a lesson, and she had instead sung them a song. Their faces lit up with surprise. She was shining on them, and they felt her shining on them, and so they shone back on her.

They asked her questions. Where do we find these stories? And Neshama told them: "They're in you, like jewels in your hearts." Why do they matter? "Because they're treasures. These memories, these images, come forth from the ground of the same wisdom we all know, but that you alone can tell."

The prisoners stared at her, mesmerized. They looked like family, and neighbors, black and white and Asian and Hispanic, all in their blue denim clothes. Some looked pissed off, some bored, some attentive; the older ones all looked like God.

When I at last got Neshama off the stage, I gave them a second round of my best writing tips.

There was warm, respectful applause. Neshama got up and told another story. It was about her late husband, and a pool he would hike to, where there was a single old whiskery fish swimming around. Neshama stripped her story down to its essence, because only essence speaks to desperate people. And the men rose to give her a standing ovation. It was a stunning moment. All she had done was tell them, "I'm human, you're human, let me greet your humanness. Let's be people together for a while."

Neshama explained her storytelling guild to them, and one of the guards sat down to listen. We did a duet, the two of us answering questions, telling the men useful stories of our own work, and the writers we love, whom maybe they would love, too, who have filled our communal well from many years and different backgrounds.

We had evoked the listening child in these men, with the only real story anyone has ever told, that the teller has been alive for a certain number of years and has learned a little in surprising ways, in the way the universe delivers truth. While I saw these men through the haze of our desire that things go well, I also saw beautiful rough glass, tumbled in the turbulent and unrelenting streams of prison life. I saw that these men looked out for one another. I saw that they had nothing but the present, the insides of their minds, glimpses of natural beauty, library books, guilt, rage, growth, and one another. I saw that these lives were of value. I had a sudden desire to send them all my books, all of my father's and friends' books, as well. Also to donate my organs.

Why did these men make me feel like being so generous? Maybe it was all the fresh air we'd brought in, the wind and the rain and ourselves. It was as if we'd come with an accordion, and as we talked and listened, the bellows filled and let breath, ours and theirs, in and out past the metal reeds.

Matches

Heroes come in all circumstances and ages. The prophet tells us, "Your old will have visions; your young will dream dreams." Elderly women in a retirement community in Mill Valley protested the war in Iraq on a busy thoroughfare with placards every Friday for years. A man I know of twenty-two, halfway to a medical degree, is pursuing ballet dreams in New York City. Some people my age—extreme middle age—train for marathons, or paddle down the Amazon, or skydive, or adopt. They publish for the first time.

Me? I may have done the most heroic thing of all. I went on match.com for a year.

The thing was, I had just done something

brave, which was to write a memoir with my son, tour the East Coast with him, and appear on stages before hundreds of people at a time. But one dream coming true doesn't mean you give up on other lifelong dreams. You're not dream-greedy to want, say, a cool career and a mate. And having realized this one long-shot dream with my grown child gave me the confidence to try something even harder: to date.

I recoil even from the word "date," let alone the concept of possibly beginning a romantic relationship. Those woods are so spooky. I have an almost perfect life, even though I've been single since my last long-term boyfriend and I broke up four years ago. I really do, insofar as that is possible in this vale of tears—a cherished family, a grandchild, church, career, sobriety, two dogs, daily hikes, naps, perfect friends. But sometimes I am lonely for a partner, a soul mate, a husband.

I had loved the sleeping-alone part. I rarely missed sex: I had tiny boundary issues in all those years of drinking, and by my early twenties I had used up my lifelong allotment. I overserved myself. I do love what Wodehouse called the old oompus-boompus when it happens to be in progress, but wouldn't go out of my way. Additionally, I have spent approximately 1,736 hours of this one precious life waiting for the man to finish and pretending that felt good. And I want a refund.

What I missed was checking in all day with my person, daydreaming about him, and watching TV together at night. There, I've said it: I wanted someone to text all day and watch TV with.

I am skittish about relationships, as most of the marriages I've seen up close have been ruinous for one or both parties. In four-fifths of them, the men want to have sex way more often than the women do. I would say almost none of the women would care if they ever got laid again, even when they are in good marriages. They do it because the man wants to. They do it because it makes the men like them more, and feel close for a while, but women love it mostly because they get to check it off their to-do lists. It means they get a pass for a week or two, or a month.

It is not on the women's bucket lists. I'm sorry to have to tell you this.

Also, ninety-one percent of men snore loudly— badly, like very sick bears. I would say that CPAP machines are the greatest advance in marital joy since the vibrator. They transform an experience similar to sleeping next to a dying silverback gorilla into something like sleeping next to an aquarium.

And the women are not crazy about the men's secret Internet-porn lives. But perhaps we will discuss this at another time.

Yet union with a partner—someone with whom to wake, whom you love, and talk with on and off all day, and sit with at dinner, and watch TV and movies with, and read together in bed with, and do hard tasks with, and are loved by. That sounds really lovely.

I had experienced varying degrees of loneliness since my guy and I split up. After our breakup, I had just assumed there would be a bunch of kind, brilliant, liberal, funny guys my age to choose from. There always had been before. Surely my friends would set me up with their single friends, and besides, I am out in the public a lot doing events at bookstores and political gatherings, the ideal breeding ground for my type of guy. But I hadn't met anyone.

People don't know single guys my age who are looking for single women my age. A sixty-year-old man does not fantasize about a sixty-year-old woman. A seventy-year-old man might. And an eighty-year-old—ooh-la-la.

Almost everybody wonderful whom my friends know is in a relationship, or gay, or cuckoo.

I went onto match.com with a clear knowledge that relationships are not the answer to lifelong problems. They're hard, after the first trimester. People are damaged and needy and narcissistic. I sure am. Also, most men a single woman meets have been separated or divorced for about twenty minutes.

The man of my most recent long-term relationship, whom I'd been with nearly seven years, was in a new, committed relationship about three weeks after we split up. I am not kidding. You can ask him. We're very friendly.

So I signed up at match.com. This—subscribing—means you can communicate with people at the site, instead of just studying the profiles, questionnaires, preferences, and photographs for free. I subscribed and answered the questions.

My preferences are: smart, funny, kind; into nature, God, reading, movies, pets, family, liberal politics, hiking; I prefer sober, or sober-ish.

So the first morning, eight profiles of men varying in age from fifty-four to sixty-three arrived by e-mail. Most seemed pretty normal, with college degrees, which I don't have, but certainly meant to; some attractive; mostly divorced, but some, like me, never married; some witty, some dull, some bizarre; sort of like real life.

Curiously, almost without exception, they were "spiritual but not religious." I thought for a while that this meant ecumenical, drawn to Rumi, Thomas Merton, Mary Oliver. But I have come to learn that this means they think of themselves as friendly. They are "glass-half-full kind of people." That's very nice. They like to think that they are "closest to Buddhism" and "open to the magic that is all around us." They are "people people." They are "open-minded and welcome all viewpoints." They are rarely seeking religious nuts like me— rather, they are seeking open, nonjudgmental women. (The frequent reference to wanting a non-judgmental woman makes a girl worry. What if you're pretty nonjudgmental, but then Tiger Woods asks you out for coffee, or Phil Spector, and little by little, more is revealed?) A strangely high number of them mention that they hope you've left your baggage at the airport—because, I guess, they are all well! How great. I love this so much.

Eight new guys arrived every day, along with a remnants section of men who lived pretty far away. Some of my eight guys were handsome, if you could believe their profiles, and in my case the profiles tended to be pretty honest. They mentioned that they drank moderately, or never, or socially (the most you can admit to; there is no way to check for "drinks alcoholically").

For my maiden voyage, I had coffee with an accomplished local man, who said his last girlfriend had been religious, a devout Jew, and this had driven him crazy. I said I was probably worse. We parted with a hug.

I selected a nice-looking Englishman with grown children for my second date. He said he had a good sense of humor, loved movies. He was, perhaps, the tiniest bit fat. I don't care much about weight, or hair loss. I e-mailed, and we arranged to meet at a Starbucks halfway between our homes, on a Sunday morning before my church.

This is a true story: He was ten minutes late, and shaken; he had just seen a fatal motorcycle accident on the Richmond–San Rafael Bridge. He had stopped to inspect the body, because he was worried that it was his son, although his son rode a dramatically different brand of motorcycle. He had gotten out, talked to the police, and taken a peek at the corpse. This sort of put the kibosh on things for me. I recommended that we reschedule to a day when he hadn't seen any dead people. He wanted to proceed. I got him a nice cup of tea.

I liked him, though, and we exchanged adorable and kicky e-mails, arranging another date, for sushi, and he was lively, cultured, and sort of charming in his e-mails and texts. But at lunch, during the first forty-five minutes of the conversation, he accidentally forgot to ask me anything about my life. It was fascinating, that we did not get around to me until that one question. Then I got cut off.

My pointing this out politely in an e-mail the next day did not sit well.

The next guy was highly cultured, a creative venture capitalist who was familiar with my work, and he turned out to be a truly excellent conversationalist. We had a coffee date, a long walk on the beach, a candlelit dinner, texts and e-mails in between, definite chemistry, and then I didn't hear from him for five days. If I wanted to go for five days without hearing from a man with whom I had chemistry and three almost perfect dates, I would repeat junior high.

My friends were great. They turned on the man immediately. (Of course, I talked mostly to my single friends and to Sam about match.com.) They knew how brave it was of me to go on dates. I was their role model.

This pattern repeated—a flurry of dates, followed by radio silence on the man's part—and made me mourn the old days, when you met someone with whom you shared interests, chemistry, a sense of humor, and you started going out. After a while—okay, who am I kidding, sometimes later that day—you went to bed with him, and then woke up together, maybe shyly, and had a morning date. Then you made plans to get together that night, or the next, or over the weekend.

But that is the old paradigm. Now, if you have a connection with a match.com man, he might have nice connections with two or three other match .com women, and so each date and new dating level—coffee, a walk, lunch, and then dinner—is like being on a board game, different-colored game pieces being moved along the home path in Parcheesi.

Every few weeks, I went out with a new man and practiced my dating skills—i.e., listening, staying open, and bringing the date to a friendly close. My son has "We don't give up" tattooed on his forearm, which is sort of our family motto. So I didn't give up, even when that day's date had an unbuttoned tropical shirt, or explained that there is no real difference between Republicans and Democrats.

Sam told me not to give up, that I would meet a guy who was worthy of me, quote unquote. That made the whole year worthwhile.

One of the bad coffee dates was a kingly little man who bore an unfortunate resemblance to Antonin Scalia, complete with tasseled loafers, and was snotty and disappointed until he figured out that I was a real writer. Then he wanted to be my BFF.

I saw the profile of a handsome religious man, who had graduate degrees and a great sense of humor and did not look like Antonin Scalia. He said he believed in courtesy and friendliness. Okay, I'll bite. The only iffy answer on his questionnaire was that he was "middle of the road."

I dropped him a line.

He wrote back fifteen minutes later. "Your politics are abhorrent to me."

I loved that. "Middle of the road" almost always means conservative, I promise. It means the person is Tea Party but would consent to getting laid by a not-hysterical liberal, which rules me out.

A man with a graduate degree, a great sense of humor, spiritual but not religious, wrote to say he loved my work and felt we were kindred souls. We met at Starbucks. He was very sweet and open, but had a compulsive Beavis and Butt-head laugh. After ten minutes of this, my neck went out on me.

Then I met a man who was as far to the left as I am, in the weeks before the presidential election! Heaven. He was English also. I am powerless in the face of foreign accents.

Or rather, I used to be.

We went out four times in rapid succession, for coffee, lunches, a hike. We had chemistry, laughed a lot, sent lots of e-mails. But we didn't touch. I thought, in my mature and/or delusional way, that this would come, but it didn't. I made a few practice casual touches, but he didn't respond.

My consultants said that I should pay attention to this. Part of me didn't believe them—this guy knew we weren't on hikingpals.com. We both wanted mates. But then I got it, that my horrible friends were right, and he didn't feel physical with me. I felt teary and surprised. I wrote to him, with my e-mail voice high in my throat, saying that maybe it wasn't going to happen, and maybe we should take a break while I went out of town.

He said he wanted to pursue this and for me not to throw in the towel.

Hooray. My heart soared like an eagle. We stayed in touch by e-mail while I was gone for a couple of weeks.

I got home. He asked me out to lunch, and we had an easy, entertaining time. Afterward he wrote that he had really enjoyed it. I asked him if he wanted to go for a hike on Thanksgiving morning, before the hordes and riffraff arrived at my house. We had coffee in the kitchen with my son and younger brother, and then we had the most beautiful walk. We hiked the next morning, too. Then, in a feat of derring-do, I invited him to a movie that night and kept my adorable little starfish hand on the space where the armrest would have been, if I hadn't stealthily raised it when he went to get popcorn. But he didn't reach for my hand; and to make a long story short, we haven't seen each other since that night. After four days of silence, I wrote to say that I guessed it wasn't going to happen. He wrote back that, yes, this was probably true; it had felt friendly but not romantic.

Now he is my mortal enemy.

That was four months ago. There have been some smart, sweet guys since, even one recently. And today, I had coffee with the first guy, from almost exactly one year ago. We compared notes; he loved "Your politics are abhorrent to me," and commiserated about the second Englishman. He and I don't have huge chemistry, but he's a good guy, and it was pleasant.

You could say that my year on match.com was not successful, since I am still single, have been reduced to recycling my Starbucks companions, and am pleased with "pleasant." To have gone out so many times took almost everything I had, and then I didn't even meet the right man. You start to wonder if there's something wrong with you.

Nah.

But I have two weeks left till my membership expires. Anything could happen. God is such a show-off, and I never give up on my dreams. Plus, amazingly, I have learned how to date. I can meet guys for coffee and hang out with them for an hour, and either not have to see them again or keep my heart open, hoping I do. Talk about awesome. I did it.

Families

Sustenance

My parents were about the pursuit of the so-called good life. When they fell in love after World War II, it was as intellectuals. This meant that you went out with other couples like you—good-looking, highly educated, and ironic folks who listened to Coltrane and Miles Davis, and raised their kids to be extremely high achievers, drank a lot of wine, passed along great books, knew about the latest poets, and cooked Julia Child's recipes and cutting-edge ethnic food.

I still remember my mother fully engaged in a number of enlivening, centering pursuits—cooking, writing for local papers, reading, baths, hanging out with her best women friends making marmalade or chutney (then trying to trick the poor children into liking it). And the figs my father and I devoured from our friends' backyards—how perfectly one fit into your mouth, the succulent flesh with just a little something to chew against to keep you focused, the honey juice that didn't run down your chin but ran down your throat, bathing you in the exotic ancient pleasure of a most common fruit.

The food and life my parents created would have been delicious and nourishing, if it had not been for one tiny problem—that they were so unhappy together. My brothers and I ate cassoulet at a table where our parents avoided making eye contact and, rather than shout, which was considered déclassé, engaged in clipped conversation. It was *The Joy of Cooking* meets Harold Pinter. So the steamed persimmon pudding was easy on the taste buds but hard to swallow, because it came at such a cost: a lump in the throat, anxiety in our bellies.

What had happened that turned my parents from the bright young things who fell in love over literature and wine to a cheerless woman and man who after dinner took their books and glasses to opposite ends of the living room, connected only by a lily pad of children on the rug between them, lost in homework?

I think the answer is what didn't happen: They were not able to take their pleasures, their love of their children, out to the next concentric circle, where something bigger awaited. My mother and her women friends made not only vats of that world-class chutney but also *mole poblano* and cakes from scratch, and yet because she was empty inside and stayed in a miserable marriage for twenty-seven years, she who cooked like a dream could not ever feel satisfyingly filled and got fat.

I found the spiritual food for which I longed as a child in the families of my two best friends. One was Catholic and lived down the block. The Catholics said grace before serving up aggressively modest fare—English muffin pizzas, tuna noodle casserole, fish sticks. The parents seemed to enjoy each other's company: what a concept. Sometimes they yelled at each other and then later hugged and kissed in the kitchen—oh my God. It had never crossed my mind that peace could be found in full expression, in yelling and weepy embraces.

I also loved to eat with—and be with—a Christian Science family, who did not yell but read the Bible and Mrs. Eddy together. When I was at their house, we prayed, eyes closed, breathing deeply. In the silence you could feel and hear your own

breath in your nostrils, and that could be both re-
laxing and scary, like having a car wash in your
head. Of course, I did not mention this to my parents; they would have been horrified. For me it was
heaven, even though we frequently ate snacks for
dinner—popcorn, store-bought pie. This food was
so delicious because of the love in that house, the
love that had at its core a sweet, strong marriage.
The parents did not yell or kiss as much as the
Catholics, but I felt enveloped by the friendly confidence of their faith, and I was sad each time I was
remanded to the spiritual anorexia at my house.

By the time I was in high school, I did what
all bright perfection-seeking girls learned to do,
besides staying on my toes because something
bad might be about to happen: I dieted. Or, come
to think of it, binged, dieted, and binged, like my
mother, but never felt that simultaneous state of
being full without being stuffed. And like my
father, I began to drink a lot. Like both of them, I
had the disease called "More!" and absolutely could
not feel gently satisfied.

Nothing can be delicious when you are holding
your breath. For something to be delicious, you
have to be present to savor it, and presence is in
attention and in the flow of breath. It begins in the

mouth, my parents' preferred site of comfort, and then it connects our heads to our bodies through our throats, and into our lungs and tummies, a beautiful connective cord of air.

In the middle and late 1960s, two things came along that started to give me my life back: the counterculture and the women's movement. A beautiful hippie teacher at my small high school gave me *I Know Why the Caged Bird Sings* and then Virginia Woolf's journals, all of which I consumed like someone at a hot-dog-eating contest. My best friend, Pammy, and I together discovered Jean Rhys and *Ms.* magazine. Then I went to a women's college, and the older girls and professors gave me the Margarets, Atwood and Drabble, and the first Nora Ephron collection, and it was all like when Helen Keller discovers that Anne Sullivan is spelling W-A-T-E-R into her hand, and wants her to spell everything in the world now. I was learning the secrets of life: that you could become the woman you'd dared to dream of being, but to do so you were going to have to fall in love with your own crazy, ruined self.

I met in circles with more and more women, who, over lentil soup and Milanos, taught me about my spirit and my needs and my body. I met with mixed groups of people to strategize protests or save open space, and we gobbled down rice and beans. I showed new friends how to make my parents' cassoulets. They taught me about halvah, pomegranate wine, and massages to heal both body and soul.

Awareness dawned on me in these years that the values of my parents' lives, of the good life, were going to be part of an evolutionary journey—the marvelous food and storytelling, bookstores, hiking—along with what I found in the religious houses of my childhood friends and in churches, along with sharing the deepest truth with women in profound and very funny conversation, along with silence and meditation. God: this was so radical, and so delicious.

I am not saying that it became easy. Like learning the piano or Spanish or meditation, I had to practice and do poorly—I had to read difficult material, and then stay with it, and talk to others, and slowly start to understand. Then I had to try something else hard and worthy. I had to seek wisdom, teachers. And oh, relationships. Don't even get me started, unless I have all day to describe the total, almost hilarious inappropriateness of every fixer-upper, I mean man, I tried to get to love me. But as Rumi said, "Through love all pain will turn to medicine," not most pain, or for other people; and the pain and failures grew me, helped slowly restore me to the person I was born to be. I had to learn that life was not going to be filling if I tried to scrunch myself into somebody else's idea of me, i.e., someone sophisticated enough to prefer dark chocolate. I like milk chocolate, like M&M's: so sue me. But I no longer have to stuff myself to the gills.

I mean, not very often.

I learned from all my teachers that when I feel like shoveling in food, a man, or expensive purchases, the emptiness can be filled only with love—a nap with the dogs, singing off-key with my church. Or maybe, perhaps, a fig.

I learned that opening myself to my own love and to life's tough loveliness not only was the most delicious, amazing thing on earth but also was quantum. It would radiate out to a cold, hungry world. Beautiful moments heal, as do real cocoa, Pete Seeger, a walk on old fire roads. All I ever wanted since I arrived here on earth were the same things I needed as a baby, to go from cold to warm, lonely to held, the vessel to the giver, empty to full. You can change the world with a hot bath, if you sink into it from a place of knowing that you are worth profound care, even when you're dirty and rattled. Who knew?

Dad

No one can prove that God does or doesn't exist, but tough acts of forgiveness are pretty convincing for me. It is so not my strong suit, and I naturally prefer the company of people who hold grudges, as long as they are not held against me. Forgiveness is the hardest work we do. When, against all odds, over time, your heart softens toward truly heinous behavior on the part of parents, children, siblings, and everyone's exes, you almost have to believe that something not of this earth snuck into your stone-cold heart.

Left to my own devices, I'm a forgiveness denier—I'll start to think that there are hurts so deep that nothing can heal them. Time alone won't necessarily do the trick. Our best thinking isn't enough, or we would all be fine, instead of in our current condition. A lack of forgiveness is like leprosy of the insides, and left untreated, it can take out tissue, equilibrium, soul, sense of self. I have sometimes considered writing a book called *All the People I Still Hate: A Christian Perspective*, but readers would recoil. Also, getting older means that without meaning to, you accidentally forgive almost everyone—almost—so the book would not be long.

You forgive your mother, for having had such terrible self-esteem, dependent on being of value to all men, everywhere, in every way. You forgive her for not having risen up, for not teaching you how to be an autonomous, beautiful woman, for not teaching you how to use eyeliner and blotting papers, and for not having been able to lose the extra fifty pounds that led to childhood embarrassment and your own lifetime obsessions. You forgive your father, for—well, you know—everything. The masculine shut-downedness, for which only the Germans have a word, the faithlessness, the drinking, and the general contempt for women, with their icky, messy, mysterious bodies and minds. You forgive all but the very worst boyfriend, with whom even Jesus struggles. You forgive awful bosses, gravely incompetent doctors. You forgive your child's peers who bullied him or first got him smoking cigarettes or weed. You forgive your professional rival, especially if you surpass him in stature, and his books sell poorly, and his hair falls out, and people can finally see what a generally loathsome pervert and fraud he is, ideally in the book review section of *The New York Times*. You mostly forgive life for being so unfair, for having stolen away from and saddled us with so much, for being so excruciating to most of the world. You even semi-sort-of-mostly forgive yourself, for being so ridiculous, such a con, a nervous case, a loser.

Then, seemingly out of nowhere, a giant wound is created, revealed, reopened. Your child has grown to hate and blame you, bear false witness against you; or your sister's ex charges someone in the family with a ghastly crime to wreak revenge. Or someone steals your retirement savings. Or your ex marries an adorable, mature teenager.

I have been known to hold the random grudge, usually against a really rotten egg. Yet for two years recently I was quite mad at my dad—the person I loved best.

The problem with this is that he has been dead for thirty-four years. Also, he died tragically, way too young. So you'd think I might cut him some slack.

Nah.

I was, seriously, a perfect daughter. I got great grades for him, kept the family together, rubbed his feet, and read way beyond my years, starting at five, like a cross between a geisha and Susan Sontag. Later I could dazzle his friends with my charm. He loved this. I overlooked the weaknesses in his character, and the destruction these weaknesses wrought on our family. I made him drinks, I drank with him. I became who I am—a writer, intellectual, conversationalist—to please him.

I was twenty-three when he got sick with brain cancer in his early fifties, after which I devoted myself to his care. I hung out with him every day, because his girlfriend, D, and my older brother had jobs and my younger brother was in high school. I took him to most of his doctor appointments, chemo, radiation, for two years. I kept hope alive when his mind was still working, and then I became his hospice care and mother when it failed.

I never quite got over his death, not really, and I missed him beyond words. So much of his life

and passions—literature, hiking, birds, writing—
became mine. Except for these weaknesses of
character—wine, women, the way he'd treated my
mom—he'd been a great father, handsome and
witty to boot, like a Kennedy.

However, a few years ago I came upon a journal
he kept for the first year of his brain cancer. Actually, D sent it from the East Coast, where she lived
with her husband of thirty years, with a note saying she thought I would want to have it. She and I
had not spoken since Dad died. He had been diagnosed only one month after they fell in love, and
while we knew she'd gotten a bum deal, there
had been distance between her and my brothers
and me both while Dad was alive and after he died.

I dove into the journal, the lake of my father
being alive again, so glad to hear his voice, looking
forward to the good memories—mostly, of course,
of him and me.

But instead, he wrote about how comforting
D's company and devotion were, along with some
harsh things about me, such as how unpleasant it
was that I was sometimes so emotional. For example, I cried openly because the person I loved most
was dying so young. He wrote some things about
how I tried too hard to be brave and hopeful. He

wrote: "Annie came to the hospital, full of the usual false good cheer and bad jokes."

After reading this, I felt as though everything in the known world was now open to dispute. I was stung, shaken to my boots. I didn't even know where to start processing this. So I cut him off.

My heart was hard by the next day, when the tears stopped. I put him out, literally; I took his journal to the garage. I summoned what self-esteem I could, and anger. The hell with him. What a dead guy. Talk about losers. Seriously—dead as a doornail. I had spent my life trying to get him to honor me. I needed to get on with my own life.

Yeah, right.

Despite talking about the betrayal with my best friends, my therapist, and my younger brother, who had been barely mentioned in the journal, I could not let go of the resentment. The bruise went so deep. Besides, it was intoxicating. Resentments make even the best of us feel superior. I've always found a kind of comfort in them, as if they were wire monkey moms, a place to hold on that is better than nothing.

I passed through all the stations of the cross—the hurt, numbness, disgust, the thoughts of revenge, the reversion to Tony Soprano's childish response to his mother—"You're dead to me." This was not a recipe for self-respect, to be almost sixty, acting ten. You are so dead to me—double dead, infinity dead.

Addicts and alcoholics will tell you that their recovery began when they woke up in pitiful and degraded enough shape to take Step Zero, which is: "This shit has got to stop." Fortunately, with twenty-six years of church, twenty-five years of recovery from alcoholism, twenty years of brilliant if intermittent therapy, and the loving friends in my inner sanctum, I got to Step Zero in only a year. Well, maybe a year and a half.

Growing up is not going nearly as efficiently as I had hoped.

Finally, though, I climbed out of my hole onto Step Zero. I'd had my fill of being in the hole of self-righteousness. I was no longer willing to let this neon insult overload me and wipe out whatever other visions I might have of life, and of myself.

Somehow I had a fleeting sense of doubt that something had been *done* to me, as opposed to my father's having acted out of his own fears and compulsions, his need to convey his truth, as I had acted out of mine, and D had acted out of hers, in sending me the journal without warning me of its contents. And I mean *fleeting*, but still a crack.

The beginning of forgiveness is often exhaustion. You're pooped; thank God.

You don't get there by willpower. The readiness comes from the movement of wisdom and good will, or what maybe in a crazy moment of abandon I'd call grace. To take far loftier examples than our own, people told Robert E. Lee at Appomattox, "If you stop now, all those lives will have been in vain." But he said, "Enough. It's over." After 1945, instead of people saying, "Let's pound the Germans into the ground," the Marshall Plan came to be. Let's rebuild. Let's help our enemies rebuild, and see what happens.

Something deeply mysterious jiggles loose in us that finally says, I'm going to let it go, instead of breathing the hot little flame into a conflagration.

I was done not forgiving my father or D, though I wanted to forgive them, which was a start, but I felt like a shivering blue child being told to jump into the cold pool.

Horribly, when all you want is relief from the pain, you instead need to tune in to it, right in to the lonely clench. You need to know how much the toxin has invaded you.

So I began to breathe into the fist, like loosening a knot. I raised my eyes to my father, who actually wert in heaven, and this put him in perspective: he didn't get to be alive anymore. He had paid. What a flawed and complex person, so erudite and brilliant. Who looked at the track marks on my fifteen-year-old brother's arms and pretended not to see. And who stood vigil at San Quentin when they gassed someone. Who orchestrated a warm, active relationship between his children and his mistress, all while still married to our mother. Who took us all clamming at minus tides, dug around with trowels in the sopping sand at dawn, then made us clam chowder for dinner. Who wrote like a dream and made a living as a writer, and yet died in debt. Who betrayed his longtime mistress, with whom he'd betrayed our mother. Who lived as much as he could the Emerson line "The happiest man is he who learns from nature the lesson of worship." Who faced his death with a lot of dignity. Who was who he was who he was.

I will never know where that willingness to see him came from, although talking with friends is where most of my insight comes from. As my heart softened slightly, my gut, the seat of the pain, rose in wonder, like a brass band, and said, "Hey, wait— I support this. I support you."

Seeing him as a human provided me with the courage to stand up to the resentment and say, I'm not going to let you rob me anymore of my sense of modest generosity.

People like to say, "Forgiveness begins with forgiving yourself." Well, that's nice. Thank you for sharing. It does and it doesn't. To think you know is proof that you don't. But forgiveness sure doesn't begin with reason. The rational insists that it is right, that we are right. It is about attacking and defending, which means there can be no peace. It loves the bedtime story of how we've been injured. The rational is claustrophobic, too. The choice is whether you want to stay stuck in being right but not being free or admit you're pretty lost and possibly available for a long, deep breath, which is as big as the universe, stirs the air around, maybe opens a window.

I called on spirit, whom I usually picture as either a breeze or Isaac Stern, but this time I saw a psychiatrist with a clipboard. She listened, said, "Hmm," nodding as I spewed it all out—the wrong, the blame, the exhaustion. Hmm. If someone listens, deeply, you've been heard, which helps you absorb it, and you can lay it at the feet of the right god. You can forgo the arithmetic of adding up the damage again, lay your Bartleby ledger in your lap, and look up. Looking up is the way out. And Hmm is very close to Omm, which is the sound of the universe. Hmm, she said: good work.

I felt as if I had gotten a leg and most of one shoulder out from the bell jar. There was fresh air on my skin. Rumi wrote, "Out beyond ideas of wrongdoing and rightdoing, there is a field. I'll meet you there." In that field, you're under a wide swath of sky, so the story becomes almost illimitable, instead of two small nutty people with grievances and popguns. You have to leave your crate, though; this will not happen inside your comfort zone. But if you can make a break for that field, you might forget all the whys, the nuance, details, and colors about the story that you're sure you've gotten right, that doom you.

So you sacrifice the need to be right, because you have been wronged, and you put down the abacus that has always helped you keep track of things. This jiggles you free from clutch and quiver. You can unfurl your fingers, hold out your palm, openhanded.

At some point in the process, I remembered something my vet said years ago when my old dog Sadie was dying. He said, "Most of her is fine, and still loves being here. Very little of her is diseased." So I looked around for any healthy tissue. I'd published a novel that was a love letter to my family and D. I had honored them, captured my family's finest, funniest moments, and with this novel, my career began. I was swamped with memories unspooling backward from my father's death, through all the years, to the first time I remember him, when I was two or three, buttoning my sweater. Spooling forward through the years, walking with him as often as we could after he got sick, and how long he refused to acknowledge that his brain was damaged, even after he wrote notes to himself directly on his girlfriend's kitchen table, bypassing the need for paper or index cards, while looking as professorial as ever. Even as he combed the cats with barbecue tongs, which I am probably weeks away from doing myself, and which the cats loved. At one of his last outpatient appointments, when D and I had to support him from the car, as if he were blotto, the oncologist asked if he was having any trouble walking. My father thought this over, and said no, not that he'd noticed. Then he turned to

his girlfriend and me, puzzled by this odd question, and asked: Had *we?* We both shrugged, innocent as Little Rascals, not wanting to hurt his
feelings. No, no, we hadn't noticed anything.

I also had a soupçon of knowledge: You know
by a certain age that, contrary to appearances, all
of us are weird, with our squinchiness, jabs, denial,
judgment, tone deafness, and we can also be so
lovely that it breaks your heart.

Months after the journal arrived, I wrote a
note to D, apologizing for how long it had taken me
to thank her for sending the journal. I sent love,
and meant it, which was a miracle.

Forgiving people doesn't necessarily mean you
want to meet them for lunch. It means you try to
undo the Velcro hook. Lewis Smedes said it best:
"To forgive is to set a prisoner free and discover
that the prisoner was you."

I wish there'd been a shortcut, but the wound
had to be revealed to heal. Lack of forgiveness
seemed like a friend, the engine that drove my life,
with a hot little motor that was weirdly invigorat-
ing. It had helped me survive.

Some time later, D sent me photographs of her
daughters and grandchildren. I was humbled, and
glad for her. She had cared for my father at her

home for almost two years, and in our family's tiny cabin above a Pacific reef the last months. I began to feel a kind of head-tilted-to-the-side fondness for her.

I sent her photos of my brothers, my son, his son. We were out of the old equation, no longer engaging in the Rube Goldberg machine of clutch, scratch, poke, and point. I remembered her piecrusts. I remembered going on walks with her and my dad, when we'd be in the woods so early that the rabbits would still be playing poker.

Effervescent bubbles of absurdity floated in. I was no longer giving myself away to something that no longer existed, that I may have made up. Who knows how much of our stories are true? In any case, when I stopped giving myself away, my father came back. I hadn't realized how desperately I'd missed him. I mean, he was my dad.

Forgiveness is release from me; somehow, finally, I am returned to my better, dopier self, so much lighter when I don't have to drag the toxic chatter, wrangle, and pinch around with me anymore. Not that I don't get it out every so often, for old time's sake. But the trapped cloud is no longer nearly so dark or dense. It was blown into wisps, of smoke, of snow, of ocean spray.

Ashes

Ash Wednesday came early this year. It was supposed to be about preparation, about consecration, about moving toward Easter, toward resurrection and renewal. It offers us a chance to break through the distractions that keep us from living the basic Easter message of love, of living in wonder rather than doubt. For some people, it is about fasting, to symbolize both solidarity with the hungry and the hunger for God. (I, on the other hand, am not heavily into fasting: the thought of missing even a single meal sends me running in search of Ben & Jerry's Mint Oreo.)

There are many ways to honor the day, but as far as I know, there is nothing in Scripture or tradition setting it aside as the day on which to attack

one's child and then to flagellate oneself while
the child climbs a tree and shouts down that he
can't decide whether to hang himself or jump,
even after it is pointed out nicely that he is only
five feet from the ground.

But I guess every family celebrates in its
own way.

Let me start over. You see, I tried at breakfast
to get Sam interested in Ash Wednesday. I made
him cocoa and gave a rousing talk on what it all
means. We daub our foreheads with ashes, I explained, because they remind us of how much we
miss and celebrate those who have already died.
The ashes remind us of the finality of death. As the
theologian said, death is God's no to all human
presumption. We are sometimes like the charac-
ters in *Waiting for Godot*, where the only visible
redemption is the eventual appearance in Act Two
of four or five new leaves on the pitiful tree. On
such a stage, how can we cooperate with grace?
How can we open ourselves up to it? How can we
make room for anything new? How can we till the
field? And so people also mark themselves with
ashes to show that they trust in the alchemy God
can work with those ashes—jogging us awake,

moving us toward greater attention and openness and love.

Sam listened very politely to my little talk. Then, when he thought I wasn't looking, he turned on the TV. I made him turn it off. I explained that in honor of Ash Wednesday we were not watching cartoons that morning. I told him he could draw if he wanted, or play with Legos. I got myself a cup of coffee and started looking at a book of photographs. One in particular caught my eye immediately. It was of a large Mennonite family, shot in black-and-white: a husband and wife and their fifteen children gathered around a highly polished oval table, their faces clearly, eerily reflected in the burnished wood. They looked surreal and serious; you saw in those long, grave faces echoes of the Last Supper. I wanted to show the photograph to Sam. But abruptly, hideously, Alvin and the Chipmunks were singing "Achy Breaky Heart" in their nasal demon-field way—on the TV that Sam had turned on again.

And I just lost my mind. I thought I might begin smashing things. Including Sam. I shouted at the top of my lungs, and I used the word "fucking," as in "goddamn fucking TV that we're getting rid of," and I grabbed him by his pipe-cleaner arm and jerked him in the direction of his room, where he spent the next ten minutes crying bitter tears.

It's so awful, attacking your child. It is the worst thing I know, to shout loudly at this fifty-pound being with his huge trusting brown eyes. It's like bitch-slapping E.T.

I did what all good parents do: calmed down enough to go apologize and beg for his forgiveness, while simultaneously expressing a deep concern about his disappointing character. He said I was the meanest person on earth next to Darth Vader. We talked, and then he went back to his drawing. I chastised myself silently while washing breakfast dishes, but then it was time for school and I couldn't find him anywhere. I looked everywhere in the house, in closets, under beds, and finally I heard him shouting from the branches of our tree.

I coaxed him down, dropped him off at school, and felt terrible all day. Everywhere I went I'd see businessmen and businesswomen marching purposefully by with holy ashes on their foreheads. I couldn't go to church until that night to get my own little ash *tilak*, the reminder that I was forgiven. I thought about taking Sam out of school so that I could apologize some more. But I knew just enough to keep my mitts off him. Now, at seven years old, he is separating from me like mad and has made it clear that I need to give him a little bit more room. I'm not even allowed to tell him I love him these days. He is quite firm on this. "You tell me you love me all the time," he explained recently, "and I don't want you to anymore."

"At all?" I said.

"I just want you to tell me that you like me."

I said I would really try. That night, when I was tucking him in, I said, "Good night, honey. I really like you a lot."

There was silence in the dark. Then he said, "I like you, too, Mom."

So I didn't take him out of school. I went for several walks, and I thought about ashes. I was sad that I am an awful person, that I am the world's meanest mother. I got sadder. And I got to thinking about the ashes of the dead.

Twice I have held the ashes of people I adored— my dad's, my friend Pammy's. Nearly twenty years ago I poured my father's into the water near Angel Island, late at night, but I was twenty-five years old and very drunk at the time and so my grief was anesthetized. When I opened the box of his ashes, I thought they would be nice and soft and, well, ashy, like the ones with which we anoint our foreheads on Ash Wednesday. But human ashes are the grittiest of elements, like not very good landscaping pebbles. As if they're made of bones or something.

I tossed a handful of Pammy's into the water way out past the Golden Gate Bridge during the day, with her husband and family, when I had been sober several years. And this time I was able to see, because it was daytime and I was sober, the deeply contradictory nature of ashes—that they are both so heavy and so light. They're impossible to let go of entirely. They stick to things, to your fingers, your sweater. I licked my friend's ashes off my hand, to taste them, to taste her, to taste what was left after all that was clean and alive had been consumed, burned away. They tasted metallic, and they blew every which way. We tried to strew them off the side of the boat romantically, with seals barking from the rocks onshore, under a true-blue sky, but they would not cooperate. They rarely will. It's frustrating if you are hoping to have a happy ending, or at least a little closure, a movie moment when you toss them into the air and they flutter and disperse. They don't. They cling, they haunt. They get in your hair, in your eyes, in your clothes.

By the time I reached into the box of Pammy's ashes, I had had Sam, so I was able to tolerate a bit more mystery and lack of order. That's one of the gifts kids give you, because after you have a child, things come out much less orderly and rational than they did before. It's so utterly bizarre to stare into the face of one of these perfect beings and understand that you (or someone a lot like you) grew them after a sweaty little bout of sex. And then, weighing in at the approximate poundage of a medium honeydew melon, they proceed to wedge open your heart. (Also, they help you see that you are as mad as a hatter, capable of violence just because Alvin and the Chipmunks are singing when you are trying to have a nice spiritual moment thinking about ashes.) By the time I held Pammy's ashes in my hand, I almost liked that they grounded me in all the sadness and mysteriousness; I could find comfort in that. There's a kind of sweetness and attention that you can finally pay to the tiniest grains of life after you've run your hands through the ashes of someone you loved. Pammy's ashes clung to us. And so I licked them off my fingers. She was the most robust and luscious person I have ever known.

Sam went home after school with a friend, so I

saw him for only a few minutes later, before he went off to dinner with his Big Brother Brian, as he does every Wednesday. I went to my church. The best part of the service was that we sang old hymns a cappella. There were only seven besides me, mostly women, some black, some white, mostly well over fifty, scarves in their hair, lipstick, faces like pansies and cats. One of the older women was in a bad mood. I found this very scary, as if I were a flight attendant with one distressed passenger who wouldn't let me help. I tried to noodge her into a better mood with flattery and a barrage of questions about her job, garden, and dog, but she was having none of it.

This was discouraging at first, until I remembered another woman at our church, very old, from the South, black, who dressed in ersatz Coco Chanel outfits, polyester sweater sets, Dacron pillbox hats. They must have come from Mervyn's and Montgomery Ward, because she didn't have any money. She was always cheerful—until she turned eighty and started going blind. She had a great deal of religious faith, and everyone assumed that she would adjust and find meaning in her loss— meaning and then acceptance and then joy—and we all wanted this because, let's face it, it's so inspiring and such a relief when people find a way to bear the unbearable, when you can organize things so that a small miracle appears to have taken place and that love has once again turned out to be bigger than fear and death and blindness. But this woman would have none of it. She went into a deep depression and eventually left the church. The elders took communion to her in the afternoon on the first Sunday of the month—homemade bread and grape juice for the sacrament, and some bread to toast later—but she wouldn't be part of our community anymore. It must have been too annoying to have everyone trying to manipulate her into being a better sport than she was capable of being. I always thought that was heroic of her: it speaks of such integrity to refuse to pretend that you're doing well just to help other people deal with the fact that sometimes we face an impossible loss.

Still, on Ash Wednesday I sang, of faith and love, of repentance. We ripped cloth rags in half to symbolize our repentance, our willingness to tear up the old pattern and await the new; we dipped our own fingers in ash and daubed it on our foreheads. I prayed for the stamina to bear mystery and stillness. I prayed for Sam to be able to trust me and for me to be able to trust me again, too.

When I got home, Sam was already asleep. Brian had put him to bed. I wanted to wake him up and tell him that it was okay that he wouldn't be who I tried to get him to be, that it was okay that he didn't cooperate with me all the time—that ashes don't, old people don't, so why should little boys? But I let him alone. He was in my bed when I woke up the next morning, over to the left, flat and still as a shaft of light. I watched him sleep. His mouth was open. Just the last few weeks, he had grown two huge front teeth, big and white as Chiclets. He was snoring loudly for such a small boy.

I thought again about that photo of the Mennonites. In the faces of those fifteen children, reflected on their dining room table, you could see the fragile ferocity of their bond: it looked like a big wind could come and blow away this field of people on the shiny polished table. And the light shining around them where they stood was so evanescent you felt that if the reflections were to go, the children would be gone, too.

More than anything else on earth, I do not want Sam ever to blow away, but you know what? He will. His ashes will stick to the fingers of someone who loves him. Maybe his ashes will blow that person into a place where things do not come out

right, where things cannot be boxed up or spack-
led back together, but where somehow that person
can see, with whatever joy can be mustered, the
four or five new leaves on the formerly barren tree.

"Mom?" he called out suddenly in his sleep.

"Yes," I whispered, "here I am," and he slung
his arm toward the sound of my voice, out across
my shoulders.

This Dog's Life

Having a good dog is the closest some of us are ever going to come to knowing the direct love of a mother or God, so it's no wonder it knocked the stuffing out of me and Sam when Sadie died. I promised Sam we'd get another puppy someday, but secretly decided not to ever get another dog. I didn't want to hurt that much again, if I could possibly avoid it. And I didn't want my child's heart and life to break like that again. But you don't always get what you want; you get what you get. This is a real problem for me. You want to protect your child from pain, and what you get instead is life, and grace. And while theologians insist that grace is freely given, the truth is that sometimes you pay through the nose. And you can't pay your child's way.

We should never have gotten a dog to begin with—they all die. I know this sounds sort of negative and bitter, but it happens to be true. It's so subversive when artists make art that will pass away in the fullness of time, or later that same day; but it's not as ennobling when your heart is broken by the death of a pet.

When Sam was two and George Herbert Walker Bush was president, I noticed I was depressed and afraid a lot of the time. I decided that I needed to move, marry an armed man, or find a violent but well-behaved dog. I was determined, as I am now, to stay and fight, and the men I tended to love were not remotely well enough to carry guns, so I was stuck with the dog idea.

For a while I called people who were advertising dogs in the local paper. People said they had perfect dogs, but perfect for whom? Quentin Tarantino? One dog we auditioned belonged to a woman who said her dog adored children, but it actually lunged at Sam, snarling. Other dogs snapped at us. One ran to hide, peeing as she ran. So I took the initiative and ran an ad for a mellow,

low-energy guard dog, and the next day we got a call from a woman who said she had just the dog.

As it turned out, she did have a great dog, a gorgeous two-year-old named Sadie, half black Lab, and half golden retriever. She looked like a black Irish setter. I always told people she was like Jesus in a black fur coat or Audrey Hepburn in Blackglama, elegant and loving and silly; such a lady.

She was very shy at first. Our vet said she must have been abused as a puppy, because she was very worried about not pleasing us. He taught us how to get on the floor with her and plow into her slowly, so that she would see that we meant her no harm— that we were in fact playing with her. She tried to look nonchalant, but you could see she was alarmed. She was eager to please, though, and she learned to play, politely.

She lived with us for more than a decade, saw us through great joy and great loss. She consoled us through friends' illnesses, the death of Sam's grandparents. She and I walked Sam to school every day. She was mother, dad, psych nurse. She helped me survive my boyfriends and the tinny, hollow loneliness in between. She helped Sam survive his first mean girlfriend.

She'd let my mother stroke her head forever. She taught comfort.

When Sam was about to turn thirteen, she developed lymphoma. She had lymph nodes in her neck the size of golf balls. Our vet said she would live a month if we didn't treat her. Part of me wanted to let her die, so we could get it over with, have the pain behind us. But Sam and I talked it over and decided to get her half a dose of chemo; we wanted her to have one more great spring. She was better two days later. She must have had a great capacity for healing: she went in and out of remission for two years, eight seasons. Toward the end, when she got sick again and probably wasn't going to get well, our vet said he would walk us through her death. He said that even when beings are extremely sick, ninety-five percent of them is still healthy and well—it's just that the five percent feels so shitty—and that we should focus on the parts that were well, that brought Sadie pleasure, like walks, smelling things, and us.

Our vet does not like to put animals to sleep unless they are suffering, and Sadie did not seem to be in pain. He said that one day she would go under the bed and not come out, and when she did, he would give us sedatives to help her stay calm.

One day, she crawled under the bed, just as he said she would.

It was such a cool, dark cave under my bed, with a big, soft moss-green carpet. Her breathing was labored. She looked apologetic.

I called the vet and asked if I should bring her in. He said she'd feel safer dying at home, with me, but I had to go in to pick up the narcotics. He gave me three syringes full. I took them under the bed with me, along with the telephone, with the ringer off, and I lay beside her and assured her that she was a good dog even though she could no longer take care of us. I prayed for her to die quickly and without pain, for her sake, but mostly because I wanted her to die before Sam got home from school. I didn't want him to see her dead body. She hung on. I gave her morphine, prayed, talked to her softly, and called the vet. He had me put the phone beside her head and listened for a moment.

"She's really not in distress," he assured me. "This is hard work, like labor. And she has you, Jesus, and narcotics. We should all be so lucky."

I stayed beside her on the carpet under the bed, and then she raised her head to look around like a black horse, and she sighed, and then laid her head down and died.

I couldn't believe it, that she was gone, even though she'd been sick for so long. But you could feel that something huge, a tide, had washed in, and washed out again.

I cried and cried, and called my brother and sister-in-law. Jamie said Stevo wasn't home, but she would leave him a note and come right over. I prayed again, for my brother to get there before Sam came home from school, so he could take Sadie's body away, to spare Sam, to spare me from Sam's loss.

I kept looking at the clock. School would be out in half an hour.

Jamie and their dog, Sasha, arrived seventeen minutes after Sadie died. I had pulled the carpet out from under the bed. Sadie looked as beautiful as ever. Jamie and I sat on the floor nearby. Sasha is a small white dog with tea-colored stains, perky ears and tender eyes, and a bright dancing quality—we call her the Czechoslovakian circus terrier—and we couldn't resist her charm. She licked us and ran up to Sadie, licking her, too, on her face. Then she ran back to us, as if saying, "I am life, and I am here! And my ears are up at this hilarious angle!"

Stevo finally arrived, only a few minutes before Sam would get home from school. I wanted Stevo to hurry and get Sadie into the car, but it was too horrible to think of Sam catching him sneaking Sadie out, like a burglar stealing our TV. I breathed miserably, and I prayed to be up to the task. Stevo sat beside Jamie. Then Sam arrived and found us. He cried out sharply and sat on my bed alone, above Sadie. His eyes were red, but after a while Sasha made him laugh. She kept running over to Sadie, the dead, exquisitely boneless mountain of majestic glossy black dog in repose on the rug. She leapt on the bed to kiss Sam, before tending to the rest of us, like a doctor making her rounds.

Then things got wild: My friend Neshama arrived. I had called her with the news. She sat down beside me. A friend of Sam's stopped by, and his father came in, too, and slipped behind Sam on the bed like a shadow. Then the doorbell rang, and it was another friend of Sam's, just stopping by, out of the blue, if you believe in out of the blue, which I don't, and then a kid who lives up the hill came by to borrow Sam's bike. He stayed, too. It was like the stateroom scene in *A Night at the Opera*. There were five adults, four kids, one white Czechoslovakian circus terrier, and one large dead black dog.

But one of the Immutable Laws of Being

Human is that whoever shows up is the right person, or the right people, and boy, were those the
right people. Sadie looked like an island of dog,
and we looked like flotsam that had formed a ring
around her. Life, death, dogs—something in us
was trying to hold something together that doesn't
hold together, but then does, miraculously, for the
time being.

Sometimes we were self-consciously quiet, as
if we were on the floor in kindergarten and should
be stretching out and napping but the teacher had
gone out and so we were waiting.

Finally, the boys went downstairs and turned
on loud rock 'n' roll. The grown-ups stayed a while
longer. I got a bag of chocolates from the kitchen,
and we ate them, as if raising glasses in a toast. As
Sadie got deader and emptier, we could see that it
was no longer Sadie in there. She wasn't going to
move or change, except to get worse and start
smelling. So Stevo carried her on the rolled-up
carpet out to my van. It was so clumsy, and so
sweet, this big, ungainly car-size package, Sadie's
barge and sarcophagus.

We could hear the phantom sounds of Sadie
for days—the nails on wood, the tail, the panting.
Sam was alternately distant and clingy and mean,

because I am the primary person he both bangs on and banks on. I stayed close enough that he could push me away. Sadie slowly floated off.

Then, out of the so-called blue again, six months later, some friends gave us a five-month-old puppy named Lily. She is huge, sweet, and well behaved—mostly. She's not a stunning bathing beauty like Sadie was; in fact, she looks quite a lot like Walter Matthau. But she's lovely and loving and we adore her. It still hurts sometimes to have lost Sadie, though. She was like the floating garlands the artist Andy Goldsworthy makes, yellow and red and still-green leaves, connected with thorns, floating away in the current. I remember how they swirled and floated back in toward the shore, got cornered in eddies, and floated free again. You know all along that they will disperse once they're out of your vision, but they will never be gone entirely, because we saw them. They illustrate the way water is like the wind, because the leaves are doing what streamers do. So the garlands are a kind of translation of this material; autumn leaves, transposed to water, still flutter.

Mom

Part One: Noraht

In a superhuman show of spiritual maturity, I
moved my mother's ashes not long ago from
the back of the closet, where I'd shoved them a
few weeks after she died. I moved them twelve
inches forward, to the front of the closet, next to
the three small pine boxes that the pebbly ashes of
our pets arrived in last year, after they were re-
incarnated as percussion instruments. My mother's ashes were given to us in a brown plastic box,
sealed, with her name spelled wrong: Dorothy
Noraht Wyles Lamott. Only her middle name was
Norah, not Noraht. She hated the name Norah,
which I love, and she didn't go by "Dorothy," which
she also hated. She went by "Nikki," the name of a

character on a radio show that she loved as a child in Liverpool.

I've been politely angry at her most of my life, even after she died. When I put the ashes in the back of the closet, it was wishful thinking that I could be done with her. A wafting white-robed figure was not going to rise from the ashes and say, "Oh, Little One, my darling daughter, I am here now, finally."

It was not until after I moved her a foot forward, to the sacred space near the pets, that I began to pray. I prayed for my heart to soften, to forgive her and love her for what she did give me—life, great values, a lot of tennis lessons, and the best she could do. Unfortunately, the best she could do was terrible, like the Minister of Silly Walks trying to raise an extremely sensitive young girl, and my heart remained ambivalent toward her.

So I left her in the closet for two years as I worked on forgiving her for having been a terrified, furious, clinging maw of neediness and arrogance. I suppose that sounds harsh. I assumed Jesus wanted me to forgive her, but I also know He loves honesty and transparency. I don't think He was rolling His eyes impatiently at me while she was in the closet. I don't think much surprises

Him. This is how we make important changes—barely, poorly, slowly. And still, He raises His fist in triumph.

I've spent my whole life trying to get over having had Nikki for a mother, and I have to say that from day one, it was much easier to have a dead mother than the old living one, the impossible one. I called her Noraht as her *nom de mort*. I forgave her for some things, but not for others; I didn't forgive her for staying in a fever dream of a marriage, for fanatically pushing us to achieve, for letting herself go from a great beauty to a hugely overweight woman in dowdy clothes and a gloppy mask of makeup. It wasn't black-and-white: I really loved her, and took great care of her, and was proud of some heroic things she had done with her life. She had put herself through law school, fought the great good fights for justice and civil rights, marched against the war in Vietnam. But she was like someone who had broken my leg, and my leg had healed badly, and I would limp forever.

I couldn't pretend she hadn't done extensive damage—that's called denial. But I wanted to dance anyway, even with a limp. I know forgiveness is a component of freedom, but I couldn't, even after she died, grant her amnesty. Forgiveness means it finally becomes unimportant for you to hit back. You're done. It doesn't necessarily mean you want to vacation together. But if you keep hitting back, you stay trapped in the nightmare—which is the tiny problem with our Israeli and Palestinian friends. And I guess I wasn't done.

I stored her in the closet beside the pets, and her navy blue purse, which the nurses had given me when I checked her into a convalescent home nearby three months before she died. I'd pick up the ashes from time to time and say to them, grimly, "Hello, Noraht." Then I'd put them back. My life weighed twenty pounds less after she died, and it was liberating to be so angry, after having been such a good and loyal girl. But many months after her death, I still thought of her the same way I do about George W. Bush—with bewilderment that this person could ever be in charge, and dismay, and something like hatred. I decided to see if I could find some flecks of light. Friends told me to pray, and to go slowly, because otherwise, my rage was so huge, how would I be able to see fireflies in the flames? I should try to go as safely, and as deeply, as I could into the mystery of our relationship. I couldn't scatter the ashes—the box was sealed but good. So I went through her purse.

It looked like a doctor's bag, worn and dusty, with two handles, the sort of purse the actor Ruth Buzzi, of *Laugh-In* fame, might hit you with. I opened it and began pulling out Kleenex like a magician pulls endless scarves from her sleeve. It was very distressing. My mother's Kleenex was distressing to me my whole life. It always smelled like the worst of her, all her efforts to disguise herself, the makeup, her perfume and lotion and lipstick and powder, all gone rancid. Also, she'd swab you with Kleenex to clean you up, with her spit. It was disgusting. In her last years, all she did was fumble for a tissue and, finding it, not remember why she'd needed it. She almost never cried— her parents were English—so it wasn't to wipe up her tears; she drowned in those uncried tears.

Uncried tears syndrome left my mother hypervigilant, unable to settle down into herself, and— to use the psychiatric term—cuckoo.

She took the purse with her everywhere. It was a weight, ballast; it tethered her to the earth as her mind floated away. It was also health and preparedness, filled with anything you might need. For instance, there were a lot of Band-Aids. You never know when you'll need one, you know only that in this world you will. There were pads of

Post-its; they gave her confidence that she could keep track of things, if only she could remember to write things down and stick them somewhere. And then remember to look at them.

There were house keys, which made me feel such grief that I had taken away her freedom. But my mother had an unbelievable life for someone so sick with Alzheimer's and type 2 diabetes, and no money, for as long as we could pull it off. We helped her have independence and a great view, and her cat, and her friends, until the very end. When we put her in the home, her freedom was gone anyway. She had only the freedom, when the nurse left at night, to fall when she tried to get up to pee, freedom to lie in wet sheets, freedom to get stuck out on the balcony and not remember how to get back inside.

There were mirrors in her purse, so she could see that she was still there: Am I still here? Peeka-boo! There I am. There were a dozen receipts from Safeway, which was right across the street from her retirement community. She was supposed to be on a strict low-carbohydrate diet to help control her diabetes, but every single receipt was for bread and cookies, which she'd sneak out to buy when she escaped, when the nurses or I was off doing the laundry. I kind of like that in a girl. She also bought dozens of tubes of Crystal Light, that intensely flavored diet drink powder you mix with water. She must have hoped it would fly straight into her brain, like Pop Rocks, energize it like tiny Tinker Bells.

I kept putting off opening her wallet. There would be pictures inside.

There were a number of receipts from our HMO in her purse. Nurses handed them to her over time and told her to hold on to them until she was called, and so she did, because she was a good girl. She loved the nurses, and she loved her doctor, so the receipts were like love letters she'd never throw away. She had a card with the direct line of a nurse who helped her clip her terrible rhino toenails. People always gave her special things, like their direct lines, because she was so eager and dignified and needy, and everyone wanted to reward and help her. People lined up to wait on her, to serve her, her whole life.

There was also a large, heavy tube of toothpaste. Maybe she bought it one day at Safeway and never remembered to take it out of her purse. Maybe she liked people to sneak peeks of it in her purse; it said of her: I may be lost, but my breath is fresh, or could be. There were three travel-size hand lotions, a tube of lipstick, a compact, and six cards from cab companies—Safe, Friendly, Professional. Just what you need in this world. Plus, she could always get home when she got lost, which she did, increasingly.

Finally I opened her wallet. It was filled with cards. She had library cards from decades before, membership cards to the Democratic Party and the ACLU and the Sierra Club. There were two credit cards, which had expired before her mind did. She had an insane, destructive relationship with money, like a junkie. There was never enough, so she charged things, charged away a whole life, to pump herself out of discomfort and fear. She assault-shopped.

There were photos of my nephew Tyler, my older brother's son, and of Sam. She loved being a grandmother. And there was an old picture of her, a black-and-white photo from when she was twenty-one or so. She was a beautiful woman, a little like Theda Bara, the white face, the jet-black hair. She had dark eyes, full of unflinching intelligence and depression and eagerness to please. In this photo, she looks like she is trying to will herself into elegance, whereas her life was always hard and messy and full of scrabbling chaos. Her frog-stretched mouth is trying to smile, but she can't, or maybe won't, because then she would look beautiful and triumphant, and there would be no rescue, no one to help or serve or save her.

She'd kept all of her cards from the years she spent practicing family law in Hawaii, a Hawaii State Bar Association card, and her Hawaii driver's license, which expired in 1985. In the license photo, she's brown from the Hawaiian sun, soft and rosy, as if she has risen through warm water, but her eyes are afraid, like she may be about to sink to the bottom again. And she did, and clung to our necks to save her.

Her purse says, "I'm a liberal, and a grandmother, and I keep my teeth clean, and my skin soft. And in case I can't remember something, I can write it down beforehand. If I get a cut, I'll bandage it right away." Her purse made my heart ache. I threw most of the contents away—the Kleenex, the lotions, the toothpaste, and the purse itself. It was like a dusty navy blue organ she didn't need anymore. I kept the things in her wallet, even the old library cards. I glanced in one of the mirrors. It scares me how alike we look. I wear glasses now, as she did. I look tired—I am tired. Also, I have a pouch below my belly, whereas I'd always had a thin waist before. Now there's this situation down there, low and grabbable. If it had a zipper, you could store stuff in there, like a fanny pack.

When I was done, I put my mother's wallet back in the closet, next to her ashes. I said a prayer. I said to Jesus, "Here. Could you watch her a while longer?" I left the wallet there for another six months.

There was also deep happiness during that time, because I fell in love. Several months into my new relationship, I went to Hawaii with my boyfriend, even though I got *very* worried beforehand about how I'd look in a swimsuit. My therapist suggested that I rub delicious, healing lotions into my thighs, so they would feel soft and cared for, and decorate them with flower tattoos. This laying on of hands changed my life, let alone that first day in the sand. While I did not feel like Brigitte Bardot when I stepped out of my beach cover-up, I did feel prettier, which on a beach is right up there with Lourdes and Medjugorje.

One morning some time later, for no particular reason I remembered that first day on the beach—the lotion, and the paper rose tattoos. And something shifted in my obtuse and grudgy self. Maybe

I stopped resisting the truth, that I sprang from the bone of my mom's bone, only a symbol of which remained. I went and got the brown plastic box of ashes from the closet. I couldn't very well rub lotion onto it, but I sat with it in my lap for a few minutes. The pouch on my belly is nice for holding children, so I let my mother sit there. Then I decided to wrap the box in birthday paper, lavender and blue with silver stars, and I taped a picture of a red rose on it. I got a little carried away—hey, Happy Late Birthday, Noraht—because the thing was, I didn't fully forgive or accept her. I'm not wild about my stomach, either; but I get along with it better. Besides, only part of a day had passed, and I was definitely not hating her anymore. Grace means suddenly you're in a different universe from the one where you were stuck, and there was absolutely no way for you to get there on your own. When it happens—when you stop hating—you really have to pinch yourself. Jesus said, and this is not an exact quote, "The point is to not hate and kill each other today, and if you can, to help the forgotten and powerless. Can you write that down and put it by the phone?" So I picked up my mother's ashes and put them on a shelf in the living room, and stood beside them for a while.

Mom

Part Two: Nikki

My mother's ashes sat on the shelf in the living room, wrapped in festive paper, for a few weeks longer. I passed her many times a day, until at some point I was occasionally able to smile at what a handful she had been. I had long ago given up all hope of ever feeling good about having had her as a mother. She was a mix of wrathful Old Testament opinion, terrified politeness, befuddled English arrogance—Hermione Gingold meets the dark Hindu goddess Kali. And God, she was annoying. I mean this objectively. You can ask my brothers, or her sister. I used to develop Parkinson's-like tics in her presence. But over time, my heart softened, and then my mind hitched a ride. Most of who I have become is the result of both having had her as a foil and having her profound and neurotic intelligence inside me: as DNA, as memory; as all the weird lessons she taught, and the beautiful lessons, too—and they are the same.

I spent my whole life helping my mother carry around her psychic trunks, like a bitter bellhop. This great load was lifted only when she died, little by little, day by day.

For a long time, I did not miss her at all, but that damn crematory box that held her ashes remained. Slowly time softened my heart, and at some point I discovered that I had forgiven her for more and more things, although none of the big-ticket items—like having ever existed, for instance. And having lived so long. Still, the mosaic chips of forgiveness were a start. I saw snippets of progress: one day when I passed her box of ashes, I said nicely, "Hi, Mommy." I'd find myself smiling at her when I passed, as if she were sitting there in person, reading. Here is what happened next.

America went to war in Iraq, and my pastor, Veronica, gave a brilliant sermon about how, with the war raging in the Middle East, now was not the time to figure everything out, like who was to blame, or whom we would vote for. It was not the time to get a new plan together and try to push it on through. It was time to be still, to get centered, to trust what we've always trusted in: friendship, kindness, helping the poor, feeding the hungry. So, having felt scattered for much of the past two years, I took Veronica's words to heart, and began to get quiet whenever possible, to go for longer walks on the mountain, to sit in beggy prayer and fretful meditation. My mind kept thinking its harsh thoughts, but I'd distract myself from them gently and say, "Those are not the truth, those are not trustworthy, those are for entertainment purposes only." Eventually I started having quieter thoughts about my mother, to see her through what the theologian Howard Thurman called "quiet eyes." Not quiet eyes, yet, in my case. But quiet for me, and then quieter still.

Gerald May wrote, "Grace threatens all my normalities." I tell you. It had taken two years for me to bring her to the light of the living room, out of the dark, dusty closet. Now I felt that it was time to scatter her ashes with the family, to honor her. The problem was, I didn't honor her. I meant to, but all I really felt was sorry for how hard her life had been, and glad she had finally passed. This is what the elders of our church call dying—"She passed," as in, She aced her exams, or turned down the offer to renew her lease. "Oh yeah, she passed," they reassure you, and I believe, theologically, they are right on both counts.

That was where I was when Veronica urged us to be still. And when I did, I found out once again how flexible and wily the human spirit is. It will sneak out from behind the bushes like a cartoon cat and ambush you if you're not careful, trick you into giving up a teaspoon of resentment, get you to take one step back from the frozen ground. Mine was lying in wait for me the day I found a photo of my mother when she was sixty, and while my heart didn't actually leap, it hopped, awkwardly, like its shoelaces were tied together.

In the photo, she is wearing her usual bizarre mask of makeup, which I have always believed was a way of maintaining both disguise and surface tension; it had humiliated me. But in this one picture, instead of feeling humiliated, I could finally see what she was shooting for: to appear beautiful and worthy, a vigorous woman on this earth. She is posing in front of a vase of flowers, clasping one wrist with her other hand, as if trying to take her own pulse. She had been divorced for eight years or so by then. One of her eyebrows is arched, archly, as though one of us had once again said something dubious or socially unacceptable. One-third of her is in darkness, two-thirds of her is in light, which pretty much says it.

You can see what a brave little engine she was, even though she'd lost everything over the years— her husband, her career, her health. But she still had her friends and family, and she stayed fiercely loyal to liberal causes, and to underdogs. And I thought, Well, I honor that, so we'll start there.

The next thing I knew, I had called my relatives, most of whom still live in the Bay Area, where we all grew up, and invited them to dinner on my mom and her twin's birthday, to scatter her ashes. Those ashes of hers were up against a lot—that our lives were better since her death—but I believed that if we released her, this would release us; and she could release herself. Releasing her would crack my hard shell, and some of the Easter-egg dye of my mother might remain, in beautiful veins. Or else I would have a complete breakdown and start to drink again, and Sam and I would have to go live at the rescue mission. What I knew was that it was the next right thing to do.

Two weeks later, three aunts, an uncle, half a

dozen cousins, my brother and sister-in-law, Sam's six-year-old second cousin, Dallas, and Gertrud, my mother's lifelong best friend, came to dinner at my house. I adore these people. I have also had fights with some of them over the years, have said terrible things, have been accused by one of them of great wrongs, for which I would never be forgiven. We've had the usual problems: failed marriages, rehab, old resentments, miserable lumpy family secrets, so much harshness and intensity. But if I had the time, I could tell you all the ways we have loved and cared for one another over the years. We're just another motley American family, still enduring. At holiday time, my friend Neshama's father-in-law used to look around at his family, shake his head, and say, "We are a bum outfit." I love that.

After dinner, we hiked up the hill to the open space closest to my house. One of my aunts, who told me to say she is fifty-four, totters when she walks now, and needs arms to hold on to. Dallas glommed on to Sam, who dragged him along like carry-on luggage, rolling his eyes but pleased. The wind was really blowing, and the sun was starting to go down. Sam and Dallas tore to the top of the hill, while the rest of us took one another's arms, blown and buffeted by the wind, walking in a doddering procession the rest of the way.

The sun was setting behind a ghost cloud, illuminating it, imposing a circle of light over it, like a cookie cutter. There were eucalyptus trees in a circle around us at the edge of the grass, looking like they were holding down the earth, like bricks on a picnic tablecloth in the wind. The trees were the only things between us and the horizon. We could see 360 degrees above fleecy trees, golden hillsides, small towns. The wind made us feel even more exposed than usual. It was so gritty that it flayed us—but lucky us, someone pointed out, with bodies to be assailed. Dallas tore around the periphery having goof attacks, flirting with Sam.

"Does anyone want to see my fireworks?" he kept calling out. "Will anyone come and see them?"

"When we're done," his mother told him sternly. "Now leave us alone."

We stood in a circle for a few minutes. "I knew that if I asked you to come tonight, you would," I said. We all cried a little. My cousins really loved my mother. She had a sweet voice, one of them said, and was always kind to them. Gertrud said, "The nature of life is harsh, and Nikki got some terrible breaks. It wasn't fair how things turned out for her. But she did a lot of good in her life, and we will always miss her."

"Yes, we will," a couple of people said responsively, the way we do at church. My heart was suddenly heavy with missing her, even as I felt the old familiar despair that she had been my mother. I just tried to breathe.

The reason I never give up hope is that everything is so basically hopeless. Hopelessness underscores everything—the deep sadness and fear at the center of life, the holes in the hearts of our families, the animal confusion within us; the madness of King George. But when you do give up hope, a lot can happen. When it's not pinned wriggling onto a shiny image or expectation, it sometimes floats forth and opens like one of those fluted Japanese blossoms, flimsy and spastic, bright and warm. This almost always seems to happen in community: with family, related by blood or chosen; at church for me; and at peace marches.

Then my brother Stevo walked away from where we stood, and began to pry open the plastic box with a knife. "Want to see my fireworks?" Dallas cried, and his mother shushed him again. He raced about on the hillside. It was distracting, like having a puppy in church, but the sun defused my annoyance, and I remembered C. S. Lewis's wonderful observation, "We do not truly see light, we only see slower things lit by it." Except for Sam and Dallas, we were as big and slow as herd animals at a watering hole. We watched Stevo take out the bag of ashes and open it into the wind. He flung Nikki away from the sunset, and the wind caught her and whooshed her away. Of course some of the ashes blew back onto my brother, and onto Gertrud, who stood beside him scattering flowers into the plume. Ashes always stick and pester you long after you have scattered them; my brother looked like he'd been cleaning a fireplace.

Then Dallas called out again, "Want to see my fireworks now? Doesn't anyone want to see my fireworks?" We all turned back toward the sun, where he stood, and gave him the go-ahead. He reached into his pockets, withdrawing fists full of something, and looking at us roguishly, he flung whatever he held up into the air. It turned out to be tiny pebbles, but because he tossed with such ferocious velocity, as high as he could manage in the wind, when they rained down on us in the very last of the sun, they shone.

Brotherman

We're not what we do, but what we receive. I have only now learned this, at the age of sixty, from my older brother, and I think he has just learned it from me. He turned sixty-two yesterday. The last thing I remember, he had just gotten his braces off.

When he came out of my guest room for coffee, I commented on the tufts of hair like pampas grass in his ears. He pretended he couldn't hear, cupped his ear, and shouted, "What's that?" When my darling nephew called to wish his dad Happy Birthday, I took the phone and told Tyler to speak as loudly as possible. "Your father is as deaf as a post now," I said. This is not true, although he has been nearly crippled at times over the last ten years by rheumatoid arthritis.

He is just over six feet tall, with thick gray hair and our mom's brown eyes. He's stocky and heavily muscled, although the last time he worked out was during the Carter administration.

I've really known him only a couple of years. I have always been close to my younger brother, Stevo, who helped me raise my son, but John is my prodigal brother. A lot of people are not aware that I even have an older brother, as twenty-five years ago he moved three hours away and forgot to visit us much until two years ago.

We went to visit him and his family a few times. We loved him, his wife, and his son, and having enjoyed our time together, we could all check it off the list.

His fiancée, Connie, and I celebrated his birthday by letting him sleep late and making him coffee. They had been to a prominent faith healer the day before, who they hoped could heal Connie's cancer. Today they left my house after breakfast for their weekly visit to the oncology department at UCSF Medical Center, where she is in clinical trials for stage four, metastatic, breast cancer, which is now in her liver and lungs. She has a bad attitude toward getting much more chemo, as she and my brother are to be married in May, and she hopes not to be bald or violently ill.

They are the two happiest people I see on any given day. It has crossed my mind that they do this to hurt me, but they simply love each other and God so much.

Taking bundles of stuff that is seemingly futile and painful and making it work as well as it can did not used to be John's strong suit. He was not able to do this with our family. Ours was like any other family, basically well-meaning, with lots of addictions, secrets, and mental illness. We were such a polite catastrophe that everyone's energy went to survival, self-medication, Mask Making 101, and myopia.

He was two years old when our parents brought me home from the hospital to destroy his life. He looked at me and said to Mom and Dad, "Take it back." Until my birth, he had been brilliant and precocious—speaking at two—but afterward, not so much.

The prince was deposed. Our younger brother was born five years after me. My parents were in over their heads. They might have been able to raise one child successfully. Even better, orchids, or llamas. Stevo and I were both reading by age four. John could not keep up and did not try. Instead, he did everything he could to feel better, including a lot of recklessness. He found me annoying and, with my bizarre looks, a major embarrassment. He hit me a lot. He put the barest possible energy into our family, while—this is true, if pathetic—I've spent most of my life force trying to keep us together. He moved out; I went east for college. Mom and Dad finally divorced.

When our father got sick, John would come by for dinner with Dad's girlfriend, Stevo, and me, but these were brief visits, not to be in the fray with us. We were always glad to see him, and he can be warm and affable, but he always had somewhere else to be, as he had just met and fallen in love with the woman he'd marry and live with for thirty-three years. By the end, my younger brother and I were bathing our dad, managing his catheters, keeping his mouth fresh. I would have loved not to do this, too.

Thank God all three of us were drinking and using drugs.

Any semblance of order that Stevo and I might have had came apart when our father got sick, but we had each other, and we lurched drunkenly onward. Five years later, John got clean and sober, as did Stevo and I two years later. John moved farther away.

He married the lovely woman he'd met, who was from a culture of discipline, politeness, tidiness, codified response, and ritualized appreciation. It was a perfect mesh, after a childhood in our crazy no-boundary foxhole family. He wanted mesh, not mess. We called him Brotherman behind his back, abridged from *Cat on a Hot Tin Roof*, because he was the successful son.

He got a good job in the insurance industry and bought a house with a pool. This was mind-blowing, that our reckless hippie brother had become so straight and successful, with such an impressive surface. Stevo, Mom, and I were raw, overly sensitive, needy, and broke.

Mom loved John more than life itself, and definitely more than she loved Stevo and me, who helped her shop, drove her around, and included her in our lives. What did this get us? Well, the great blessing of service, of doing the right thing, of being manic little church mice, but when John called her, she'd exclaim, "Isn't John a *love*?" She mentioned his calls every time we spoke, for weeks. "Oh, I had the nicest talk with John. Isn't he a *love?*" It was hard to take, but not his fault. Still.

His wife was sweetly distant, his child gorgeous and easy, and he got promotions, whereas Stevo and I were loving shambles, in the hearts of cousins and extended family, our lives full of irregularities and holes. But we had great kids and each other. We both had God in our lives, the greatest friends, and the hiking trails of Marin.

John and I talked on the phone every few months, and twice a year, if we were lucky, he stopped by on a kingly visit. He gave generously to our kids, his niece and nephew. He had impeccable timing, though, and while never there for regular old holidays with the aunts, uncles, and cousins, he was there for the most important occasions of state. He came to Stevo's wedding and our beloved uncle's funeral. And he happened to be there for our mother's last day on earth. So he always got written down in the guest book, and he got full credit.

Everyone went crazy if my brother John showed up, especially, I might add, me. His presence made any occasion special. Oh my God, cousin *John* was actually there.

I loved him deeply and knew he loved me, but it didn't add up to much. The way he had shamed me in childhood still hurt. I felt burned by how little he was able to help with Dad and then Mom. I did not know very much about who he was on the inside, what he felt, the price he'd paid to survive our weird, tense, Kabuki childhood.

Years ago I came upon Dag Hammarskjöld's line "Forgiveness is the answer to the child's dream of a miracle by which what is broken is made whole again, what is soiled is made clean again," and knew that this could not happen for us, that our parents were gone and John was just John. Take it or leave it. Life on life's terms.

The first sign that there was a crack in his shell was when he joined a fundamentalist church, with a thousand members and a Christian rock band. He'd always been utterly uninterested in faith, while Stevo and I were both believers. He'd converted. It seemed like an hour later he'd become a pillar of that church, a Bible teacher and youth leader. Our churches were 180 degrees apart in style and politics—he was strictly evangelical—but now when he visited, we could stay up all night to talk about Jesus, the mysteries of faith, the movement of grace all around us, and lives redeemed against all odds. He'd go back home and it would be months before we'd talk again.

John still had such a handsome, hard casing
that when God finally reached a tipping point with
him, He or She had to use a very heavy hand: John
got severe rheumatoid arthritis, which sent him to
bed for days on end during flare-ups. He cut his
work life in half, needed a cane to walk, and then a
cart for longer distances, like getting around the
Chico's Costco. Then his liver began to harden
and die off in spots. And those things he had
always kept at bay—the grimy, the real, and the
powerlessness—were now obvious aspects of his
life. The smooth ride was over.

He knew he needed something. He reached
out to God, and the next thing he knew, God, with
God's infinitely absurdist humor, gave him us, my
brother and me.

We received him without a lot of thought. We
just loved him. That was the whole story: love. He
was our big brother. It was like we had dog brains,
whatever was right in front of our noses was reality, and he was right in front of our noses. He
started coming to stay at my house for the weekend, with his dogs; when he and his wife split up,
he got two of the three little dogs, both barkers.
One is a very elegant small old lady named Allie,
who is lovely, but bossy and queenly and inconti-

nent, and the other, named Baxter, is a nervous case who has to wear a ThunderCoat to help with his anxieties, like a swaddled baby or a patient in a flannel straitjacket. I think he may have tiny continence issues, too, although Allie gets the blame. So every time John came, I had four dogs, a cat who was afraid of the strange little pee-pee dogs, one grown son, and a young grandchild. Stevo and his wife and daughter often came for dinner, and it was mercifully not at all like old-home week. It was a new constellation of Lamotts.

John, Stevo, and I have been collectively sober for eighty-four years. It's a start.

John found refuge among the people he had hurt and neglected. I still had some little grudgelets and feared he would leave us again, but the three of us were slowly growing up. That, grace, and exhaustion with myself allowed me to forgive. I did not want to keep score anymore. I always won, but got booby prizes. Annie, 17; John, 11—here's your travel mug, miss. If I hadn't let go, there would have been nothing but more shit and holes ahead, but because I did, there was possibility, of him and me connecting, deeply, impossibly. For me to whap that possibility away would have been crazier than I have the energy for these days.

Two years ago, he came for a visit, and we drove out to the coast and talked more honestly than we ever had. He confided on one of our drives that he thought his marriage might be ending, both parties ready to move on after my nephew left for college. They had been more like a business for years, raising their fine son together. There was no acrimony. So even though his marriage wasn't going to hold, family would, in the weedy, root-filled ground of his siblings. And it was good.

When we started to call him Brotherman as a term of endearment, he seemed to like it.

One night eight months ago when he was staying with me, and had sprung in his uncley way for family-night pizza, he mentioned that he was interested in a woman he knew from church, whose daughter had been in his youth group.

"Oh," my brother and I said. "Tell us about her."

He said she was beautiful inside and out, one year younger than he, with two daughters, one in her late thirties with two children, and one who was eighteen, who lived with Connie. He said that she had a great positive outlook on life, a powerful warmth, and a nice sense of humor, and most important, that they could talk all day, every day.

"She sounds perfect," I said.

"Well, there's this one thing," John allowed, "besides the fact that I'm not divorced."

Oh, well, I thought, she's just learning English, or has a glass eye, or keeps snakes. Whatever.

"She has metastatic breast cancer, that's in her liver now. She's had it for two years, and had massive chemo, twice. She was in remission, but isn't anymore."

"Ah," we said politely, although I wanted to add: Run, John, run—go, dog, go! Be her dear friend, or ditch her sorry-ass cancery self. I can't take any more, because of course it's always about me, Al Franken.

Instead, he fell deeply in love with this beautiful, warm, adorable, deeply damaged woman, and it stretched him. He was able to make a net wide enough to hold her.

He brought Connie to my house one weekend, and it was love at first sight for all of us. My four-year-old grandson fell to pieces of love in her presence. She is so pretty, buxom with snowy white hair and bright blue eyes, white teeth, long legs, and a comfortable tummy, the whole package. And she hikes as fast as I do, or at least she did until the last round of chemo. Her true beauty is inside, in her goodness, her generosity, her courage. We were doomed, all in this together now—we would help her fight tooth and nail, offer prayer support, see her in perfect wholeness.

Within two weeks of our meeting her and bonding, her doctor found tumors in her lungs.

The experts couldn't treat the lung cancer in Chico, so they sent her back to UCSF Medical Center, one of the country's great research hospitals. But she would need to live locally. When you are on clinical trials, there are endless scans, EKGs, side effects, and so on, making it necessary to be close by.

So she and John and the dogs have come for two or three nights almost every week for six months.

She is easy to be around, although she can drive you nuts, because she cannot receive without trying to make it up to you. For instance, she constantly does the dishes and puts things away. She details my kitchen as if it were a car. She says, "It's the least I can do," as if she needed to pay me back. But I often can't find what I'm looking for. When she reads this someday, I would like to mention again that we do not put our fruit in the fridge. Also, I have not seen my cheese slicer since John started bringing her around.

She simply does not complain about her lot, as

she fights to survive. I hate this. She remains hopeful, most days, that she will be healed. I want to shake her and say, "For the love of God, what's wrong with you? Whine, girl. Bitch and moan."

The morning after she found out she had metastases in her lungs, we went for a hike at Deer Park. We both see the glory of God in birds and wildflowers, and the meadows where it seems like a bear might suddenly appear, and the dappled light. The difference is that she doesn't have the dark black sense of humor that our family relied on for survival. For example, we passed a pile of feathers that morning, then the body of a finch. She said, "Poor little guy." She saw one of God's creatures called home. I saw *CSI: Birds*—to me, it looked like it had been dragged a ways, shedding feathers, as if a coyote had had it in a Hefty bag in the trunk of its car, lugging it there by its underarms: "Morty, get his feet . . ." We walked along, bumping shoulders.

Until two weeks ago, she had as bad a sweet tooth as John or I, although John indulges his like a dog, while I mostly try to stay away from sugar. They kept bringing sacks of fun-size chocolate bars, six-packs of Klondike ice cream bars. I asked them not to, begged and pleaded, but this took time for us to work through. The low point, for me, was one Saturday when I discovered in the freezer two packs of Klondike bars, which they eat after I go to bed, and Connie also had brought me a two-pound bag of M&M's. I didn't even know they made two-pound bags, and I am an aficionado. That very same weekend, I texted John from the market to say I was on my way home and ask if they needed anything. He texted back, "We're fine. Connie is baking." I clutched my head and dug my finger-nails into my forehead.

When I got home, the house was aromatic with the twenty-four mini glazed banana muffins she'd made while I was gone. Helpless and angry, I re-minded them that I was off sugar.

"Just try one," she said. I said no, thanks. I didn't want one. I can resist banana-based des-serts. My brother jovially said, "Just try one—they are Connie's specialty."

"No, thank you," I said again. But they wouldn't back off. It was *Green Eggs and Ham*. I thought I was going to have to shoot one or both of them. Finally, as God is my witness, Connie came toward me with a piece of warm glazed banana muffin and said, "This was mother's recipe!" I snatched it from her like a monkey and took a bite, then another. Then I ate several whole muffins. I had to hide the remaining eighteen or so, but luckily was able to find them in the morning and eat a few more. It took four days to get off sugar again after they left. I threw out the leftover Klondike bars.

They brought more when they came the following week.

Eventually, though, they caught on, and stopped bringing so many sweets. I in turn stopped flinching like one of the Three Stooges if they slipped up. I'm amazed by how well we are doing, as this has been a steep learning curve for all of us, and there will almost certainly be many tough days ahead. Not only did we get our big brother back, but we've ruined him a little, in the best possible way. He has softened his stance on all people; I don't think he's even an evangelical anymore, or if he is, he's not a very good one. For instance, at Christmas, I watched him fall for the transvestite emcee at the LGBT's gigantic World Tree of Hope lighting at the City Hall rotunda. He mentioned her a couple of times the next day, as a her: as Donna. He is a new man, which is what he promised God to be. He feels his infallibility, rigidness, and ridiculousness now, and he lets us be with him in that. He can look down the long dark corridor of life and know he cannot fix it with spackle or duct tape; he cannot avoid it or trick it out. It is going to get us all, maybe Connie first, but we will stick together in all this left-field love.

Airborne

Ski Patrol

Not too long ago, I was skiing in the mountains where Sam and I spend a weekend or two most winters. Nowadays, he instantly disappears with the hordes of snowboarders. I believe he is somewhat embarrassed to be seen with me: once, standing next to him and his friend at the bottom of a hill, I fell over for no reason. And in fact, the very first time we went skiing together, I skied in a strangely slow, inexorable path for a hundred feet or so, straight into a huge net at the bottom of the slope, erected to protect the small Ski Bear children from being crushed. Then I got tangled up in it, like a fish.

After Sam disappears, I usually take the chairlift to the top of the pony slope for a couple of runs, which anyone can manage. And I triumph. I roar down the slight incline, pretending to be an Olympian. Filled with confidence, I try the easiest intermediate slope, where I mostly fall or slide down on my butt for the first run, and then have a few extended runs of four or five minutes when I am actually skiing. By my second run down an intermediate slope, I am on my feet almost the whole time, skiing triumphantly for America.

But this time, as the chairlift carried me to the top of the intermediate slope, which I had just skied down, I experienced a moment's confusion, born of hormones, high altitude, and a light snow falling. I suddenly could not remember whether the stop we were approaching was the same one I had just skied down from. The chair slowed and lowered for us to disembark, and my seatmate got off and zipped away like a swallow, while I sat there torn between wanting to get off and thinking that mine was the next stop.

The chair jerked forward and resumed its ascent. I looked around for landmarks but saw only brightly colored skiers in clusters, and I was pretty sure that this was not the right stop . . . until a second later, when I realized I was mistaken—it was the right stop. By then, the chair was four or five feet off the ground and rising. But I did not let this deter me. I took a long, deep breath, wriggled to the edge of the chair, and flung myself off into the snow—flung myself, the way stuntmen fling themselves onto the back of speeding trains, or a clown flings himself from a bucking bronco, mugging bug-eyed for the crowd.

I estimate that I was five or six feet off the ground for the timeless instant of eternity before I crashed down into the snow. I landed hard, proving the theory of gravity once and for all. I was somehow still on my skis, for a moment, until I fell over.

I do not imagine anyone had seen anything like this before, someone hurtling into outer space with such force, from such a low starting point. I felt like Icarus, near death in the snow, with melting skis instead of wings.

I was immediately aware of two things: that I was not badly hurt, and that most people were pretending not to have noticed, out of kindness, or horror, or mortification. I am ever my mother's daughter, and so my first impulse was to smile with confidence to the few who were watching, wave like a politician campaigning from a rarely used horizontal position.

"I'm okay," I said to two pretty women who

came over and offered to pull me up. I continued to wave nonchalantly, as if this sort of silly thing happened to me all the time. I told them that I just needed to catch my breath. They made sympathetic cooing sounds and skied away. I sat up and leaned back on my hands in the snow.

By the time I finally stood, my hands were frozen. I was winded, ashamed, confused, bruised—grateful only that Sam hadn't seen me. He'd have died. He would have stabbed himself repeatedly in the head with his ski pole.

Just when I thought things couldn't get much worse, nausea struck, wave after wave, like morning sickness, and I thought, I'm going to throw up in the snow! Ladies and gentlemen, now for my next trick . . . I pretended to pinch my nostrils against the cold, but was actually pressing my hand to my mouth to hold back the tide. My head spun, and I prayed, Help me, Jesus, help me, the way a very old woman at my church named Mary used to pray at her most afraid and delirious, right in the middle of anything—sermons, songs: "I know my change is gonna come, but touch me now, Lord."

I don't know how long I stood there with my hand clamped to my mouth, only my poles and a frayed, patchwork faith to support me. All I knew

was that help is always on the way, a hundred percent of the time. Rumi said, "Someone fills the cup
in front of us." I know that when I call out, God will
be near, and hear, and help eventually. Of course, it
is the "eventually" that throws one into despair.
For instance, even now, I know America will be
restored again, eventually, although it is hard to
envision this at the moment, and it could take a
century or more for the nation and the world to recover from the George W. Bush years. But they
will. God always hears our cries, and helps, and it's
often a surprise to see what form God will take on
earth. In the old joke, a man whose plane crashes
in the tundra bitterly tells a bartender that God
forsook him—that he waited in vain for divine in-
tervention, and would have died in the snow . . . if
it hadn't been for some fucking Eskimos who came
by. So maybe a tall, strong man with a medical to-
boggan would be by soon, or the two pretty women,
or Jesus in earmuffs.

Instead, a short, plump woman pulled up on
skis a few minutes later. She was wearing an orange cap and an official jacket from the ski resort.

"I think I'm going to throw up," I said, so she
wouldn't get too close.

"Well, then, let's just stand here a moment,"

she said. She had acne and chapped cheeks, and small brown eyes.

"I think I might need help," I said, which is something I force myself to say every few years.

"You landed so hard. I saw you from up above."

I shook my head, bewildered, on the verge of tears. "Are you on the ski patrol?" I asked.

"Sort of. I'm here to help in non-emergency situations like this. Why don't you come with me." She stepped out of her skis and stood on my bindings so that I could step out of mine. We picked up our skis and I trudged after her through the snow.

We walked to a ten-by-ten-foot wooden shack away from the lift and went inside. It held two long benches, a folding chair, and shelves laden with first-aid equipment, bottles of water, used coffee cups, a walkie-talkie; and it was warm from a kerosene heater. There were two shabby windows, through which you could see snowy pine trees outside. The woman poured me a miniature Dixie cup of water, but my face was so cold that I couldn't get my lips to work and I dribbled water down my front like an aged, numbed-up woman at the dentist's.

She took the cup away from me. "Let's get your gloves off first," she said, and pulled them off, as gently as if they were mittens connected inside my jacket sleeves with a string.

She laid my gloves on the chair near the heater and pulled off her own. "Mine are nice and toasty," she said. "You can wear them for a while, until yours warm up. I'll be back soon—there are only a couple of us working this spot today." She went outside without gloves, her bare hands jammed into her pockets.

After a while, I stretched out on one of the benches and closed my eyes. The kerosene smelled like lacquer, and I kept feeling waves of nausea. My bones were cold. I could isolate the icy scent of pine trees that snuck in through the walls. Sometimes grace is a ribbon of mountain air that gets in through the cracks.

I practiced concentrating between the waves of nausea, the way I did when I was in labor, savoring ice chips and apple juice between contractions. Miles from home, holed up deeply alone in a smelly hut, I had the old, familiar feelings of separation: from myself, from God, and from the happy, pretty people outside.

I thought of the woman from the ski patrol with her small brown eyes. She looked like the monk seals that swim ashore in Hawaii to rest on the sand. The adult seals are six and seven feet long, and they all look like Charles Laughton. The newest tourists on the beach think they are dying and need to be rescued, but anyone who has been there even a day knows that they come onshore to rest. Pool workers from the beachside resorts arrive with yellow safety tape and traffic cones to rope off a space for the seals to rest in. The first time I came upon one in the sand, I thought it was trying to make eye contact with me—I was its last, best hope of being saved. It had sand around its eyes and lots of shark scars. Rory, my boyfriend at the time, who surfs in Hawaii every year, laughed and explained that the seals are perfectly fine, and when they are rested, they waddle back to the ocean.

This is how I feel about the world much of the time, when I am not feeling too far gone: Things are how they are supposed to be, all evidence to the contrary. Life swims, lumbers across the sand, rests; lumbers, swims, rests.

I lay there on the bench immobilized. If I had been a monk seal, I could have waddled up into a sitting position, slid off the bench, and pulled myself by my flippers back into the ocean. Rory once saw a mother monk seal teaching her pup how to rest by swimming up onto the sand for a while before slipping back into the waves. The two of them practiced over and over, then disappeared into the water. Remembering this made me miss Sam terribly. I felt discarded, and I needed for time to pass more quickly. I would be fine with life's contractions if they would simply pass when I am ready for them to, so I can be okay again and remember what, after all, I'm doing in labor. Being human can be so dispiriting. It is a real stretch for me a lot of the time.

I put my nose to a crack in the wall so I could smell the pine.

I couldn't wait any longer for the ski patrol woman to come back. Where was she? She'd *said*. She was my only real friend, and I was such a mess. Her voice was gentle and kind—"O that today you would hearken to His voice," the psalmist wrote, and "harden not your hearts." Okay, fine, I said to God, and then noticed that I was much less of a frozen mess than I'd been earlier. This was a lot. I could have sat up, but I wanted the ski patrol person to see the full extent of my suffering—if she ever in fact returned.

I thought of the people I know from church and political circles who are doing a kind of psychic ski patrol in the world, noticing when people are in trouble, refusing to look away, offering an ear and their own warm gloves to wear.

Twenty minutes later, my ski patrol woman did come back, rubbing her bare hands together.

"How you doing?" she asked. At first the enthusiasm in her voice worried me, because she sounded as if we might now move on to calisthenics. Then I could tell that she knew I was fine, better, rested. I was peaceful: she was my own private pool-worker, my own mother seal. I sat up and breathed in the fresh air from the open door.

She gave me another Dixie cup of water, and I hoisted it Germanically.

She walked over to the heater and checked my gloves. "They're all ready to wear again if you'll give me mine back."

I stood up. I felt like my old self, which is to say creaky but okay.

"I'd take the chair down," she said. "Unless you really want to ski."

I really wanted to ski. I'd already had one great run down this slope.

She made a huge fuss over me when I left, as if I'd been in an avalanche. I pulled on my gloves and headed out onto the huge white ocean of ice. I put on my skis again and headed down the slope. I glided and fell and got back up and skied little by little, the very best I could, all the way down the mountain.

Knocking on Heaven's Door

So there I was, on a plane returning home from St. Louis. Or rather, there I was in a plane at a gate at the St. Louis airport with, I think, the not unreasonable expectation that we would be in the air soon, as our flight had already been delayed two hours. I was anxious to get home, as I had not seen Sam in several days, but all things considered, I thought I was coping quite well, especially because I am a skeptical and terrified flier. In between devouring Hershey's chocolate and thirteen dollars' worth of trashy magazines, I had spent the two hours of the delay trying to be helpful to the other stranded passengers: I distributed all my magazines and most of my chocolates;

I got an old man some water; I flirted with the babies; I mingled, I schmoozed. I had recently seen what may have been a miracle at my church and had been feeling ever since that I was supposed to walk through life with a deeper faith, a deeper assurance that if I took care of God's children for God, He or She would take care of me. So I took care of people, and hoped that once we were on board, everything would go smoothly.

My idea of everything going smoothly on an airplane is (a) that I not die in a slow-motion fiery crash or get stabbed to death by terrorists and (b) that none of the other passengers try to talk to me. All conversation should end at the moment the wheels leave the ground.

Finally we were allowed to board. I was in row 38, between a woman slightly older than I, with limited language skills, and a man my own age who was reading a book about the Apocalypse by a famous right-wing Christian novelist. A newspaper had asked me to review this book when it first came out, because its author and I are both Christians— although as I pointed out in my review, he's one of those right-wing Christians who thinks that Jesus is coming back next Tuesday right after lunch, and

I am one of those left-wing Christians who thinks that perhaps this author is just spiritualizing his own hysteria.

"How is it?" I asked, pointing jovially to the book, partly to be friendly, partly to gauge where the man stood politically.

"This is one of the best books I've ever read," he replied. "You should read it." I nodded. I remembered saying in the review that the book was hard-core right-wing paranoid anti-Semitic homophobic misogynistic propaganda—not to put too fine a point on it. The man smiled and went back to reading.

I couldn't begin to guess what country the woman was from, although I think it's possible that she had one Latvian parent and one Korean. She sounded a little like Latka Gravas, the Andy Kaufman character on *Taxi*, except after things began to fall apart, when she sounded just like the Martians in *Mars Attacks!* "Ack ack ack!" she'd cry. But I'm getting ahead of myself.

As we sat there on the runway, the man with the book about the Apocalypse commented on the small gold cross I wear.

"Are you born again?" he asked, as the plane left the gate. He was rather prim and tense, maybe a little like David Eisenhower with a spastic colon. I did not know how to answer for a moment.

"Yes," I said. "I am."

My friends like to tell one another that I am not really a born-again Christian. They think of me more along the lines of that old Jonathan Miller routine: "I'm not really a Jew—I'm Jew-ish." They think I am Christian-ish. But I'm not. I'm just a bad Christian. A bad born-again Christian. And certainly, like the apostle Peter, I am capable of denying it, of presenting myself as a sort of leftist liberation theology enthusiast and maybe sort of a vaguely Jesusy bon vivant. But it's not true. And I believe that when you get on a plane, if you start lying you are totally doomed.

So I told the truth: that I am a believer, a convert. I'm probably about three months away from slapping an aluminum Jesus-fish on the back of my car, although I first want to see if the application or Stickum in any way interferes with my lease agreement. And believe me, all this boggles even my mind. But it's true. I could go to a gathering of foot-wash Baptists and, except for my dreadlocks, fit right in. I would wash their feet; I would let them wash mine.

But as the plane taxied out farther, the man on

my right began telling me how he and his wife were home-schooling their children, and he described with enormous acrimony the radical, free-for-all, feminist, touchy-feely philosophy of his county's school system, and I knew instantly that this description was an act of aggression against me—that he was telepathically on to me, could see that I was the enemy, that I would be on the same curling team in heaven as Tom Hayden and Vanessa Redgrave. And then the plane braked to a stop.

We all looked around for a moment, before the captain came on the PA system and announced calmly that two passengers wanted to get off the plane, right then and there. We were headed back to the gate. "What?" we all cried. The good news was that this was going to take only a minute or so, since in the past two hours we had traveled only about five hundred feet. The bad news was that FAA regulations required that security go over all the stowed luggage to make sure these two people had not accidentally left behind their pipe bombs.

The Latvian woman stared at me quizzically. I explained very slowly and very loudly what was going on. She gaped at me for a long moment. "Ack," she whispered.

Eventually the three of us in row 38 began to read. The other two seemed resigned, but I felt frantic, like I might develop a blinky facial tic at any moment. Time passed underwater.

An hour later the plane finally took off.

We, the citizens of row 38, all ordered sodas. The Latvian woman put on a Walkman and listened with her eyes closed; the Christian man read his book about the Apocalypse; I read *The New Yorker*. Then the seat-belt sign came on, and the pilot's voice was back over the PA. "I'm afraid we are about to hit some heavy turbulence," he said. "Please return to your seats."

The next minute the plane was bouncing around so hard that we had to hold on to our drinks. "Ack ack ack!" said the Latvian, grabbing for her Sprite.

"Everyone take your seat," the pilot barked over the PA system. "We are in for some rough going." My heart thumped around my chest like a tennis shoe in the dryer.

The plane rose and fell and shook, and the pilot came back on and said sternly, like an angry dad, "Flight attendants, sit down now!" The plane hit huge waves and currents on the choppy sea of sky, and we bounced and moaned and gasped.

"Whhhoooooaaaa!" everybody said as one, as though we were on a roller-coaster ride. We're going down, I thought. I know that a basic tenet of the Christian faith is that death is really just a major change of address, but I had to close my eyes to squinch back tears of terror and loss. Oh my God, I thought, oh my God: I'll never see Sam again. This will kill me a second time. The plane bucked and shook without stopping, and the Christian man read calmly, stoically, rather pleased with his composure, it seemed to my tiny, hysterical self. The Latvian closed her eyes and turned up her Walkman. I could hear it softly. And I, praying for a miracle, thought about the miracle I had seen in church one Sunday.

One of our newer members, a man named Ken, is dying of AIDS, disintegrating before our very eyes. He came in a year ago with a Jewish woman who is with us every week, although she does not believe in Jesus. Shortly after Ken started coming, his partner, Brandon, died of AIDS. A few weeks later Ken told us that right after Brandon died, Jesus had slid into the hole in his heart left by Brandon's loss, and had been there ever since. Ken has a totally lopsided face, ravaged and emaciated, but when he smiles, he is radiant. He looks like

God's crazy nephew Phil. He says that he would gladly pay any price for what he has now, which is Jesus, and us.

There's a woman in the choir named Ranola, who is large and beautiful and jovial and black and as devout as can be, who has been a little standoffish toward Ken. She has always looked at him with confusion, when she looks at him at all. Or she looks at him sideways, as if she wouldn't have to quite see him if she didn't look at him head-on. She was raised in the South by Baptists who taught her that his way of life—that he—was an abomination. It is hard for her to break through this. I think she and a few other women at church are, on the most visceral level, a little afraid of catching the disease. But Ken has come to church most Sundays for the past year and won over almost everyone. He missed a couple of Sundays when he got too weak, and then a month ago he was back, weighing almost no pounds, his face even more lopsided, as if he'd had a stroke. Still, during the Prayers of the People, he talked joyously of his life and his decline, of grace and redemption, of how safe and happy he feels these days.

So on this one particular Sunday, for the first hymn, the so-called Morning Hymn, we sang

"Jacob's Ladder," which says, "Every rung goes higher, higher," while, ironically, Ken couldn't even stand up. But he sang away sitting down, with the hymnal in his lap. And when it came time for the second hymn, the Fellowship Hymn, we were to sing "His Eye Is on the Sparrow." The pianist was playing and the whole congregation had risen—only Ken remained seated, holding the hymnal in his lap—and we began to sing, "Why should I feel discouraged? Why should the shadows come?" Ranola watched Ken rather skeptically for a moment, and then her face started to melt and contort like his, and she went to his side and bent down to lift him—lifted this white rag doll, this scarecrow. She held him next to her, draped over and against her like a child while they sang. And it pierced me.

I can't imagine anything but music that could have brought this about. Maybe it's because music is about as physical as it gets: your essential rhythm is your heartbeat; your essential sound, your breath. We're walking temples of noise, and when you add tender hearts to this mix, it somehow lets us meet in places we couldn't get to any other way.

Meanwhile, little by little, the plane steadied,

and the pilot announced that everything was okay. I was so excited that we were not going to crash and that I might actually get to see Sam again that I started feeling mingly; I wanted the Christian man to be my new best friend. But just as I opened my mouth, the pilot came back once more to ask if there was a doctor on board.

A woman behind us, who turned out to be a nurse, got up and went back to investigate. The Christian man prayed; I tried to rubberneck, but I couldn't see a thing. I went back to thinking about Ken and my church and how on that Sunday, Ranola and Ken, of whom she was so afraid, were trying to sing. He looked like a child who was singing simply because small children sing all the time—they haven't made the separation between speech and music. Then both Ken and Ranola began to cry. Tears were pouring down their faces, and their noses were running like rivers, but as she held him up, she lay her black weeping face against his feverish white one, put her face right up against his and let all those spooky fluids mingle with hers.

When the nurse sitting behind us returned, she offered the news that a woman in the back was having a heart attack. A heart attack! But there were doctors on hand, and the nurse thought the woman was going to be okay.

"Good Lord," said the Christian man. We looked at each other and sighed, and shook our heads, and continued to look at each other.

"God," I said. "I just hope the snakes don't get out of the cargo hold next." The prim apocalyptic man smiled. Then he laughed out loud. The Latvian woman started laughing, although she still had her Walkman on, and while I hate to look like I'm enjoying my own jokes too much, I started laughing, too. The three of us sat there in hysterics, and when we were done, the man reached over and patted the back of my hand, smiling gently. The Latvian woman leaned in close to me, into my Soviet airspace, and beamed. I leaned forward so that our foreheads touched for just a second. I thought, I do not know if what happened at church was an honest-to-God little miracle, and I don't know if there has been another one here, the smallest possible sort, the size of a tiny bird, but I feel like I am sitting with my cousins on a plane seven miles up, a plane that is going to make it home— and this made me so happy that I thought: This is plenty of miracle for me to rest in now.

Dear Old Friend

We turn toward love like sunflowers, and then the human parts kick in. This seems to me the only real problem, the human parts—the body, for instance, and the mind. Also, the knowledge that every person you've ever loved will die, many badly, and too young, doesn't really help things. My friend Marianne once said that Jesus has everything we have, but He doesn't have all the other stuff, too. And the other stuff leaves you shaking your sunflower head, your whole life through.

I got a message to call my aunt Gertrud last week. She is not my blood aunt, but was adopted when I was two. She and her husband, Rex, were my parents' best friends my entire life, our two families eventually part of one whole. She became Sam's grandmother one month after conception; neither of her children decided to have kids.

I remind her whenever she nags me about something that I ruined my figure to give her a grandson.

She and I stick together.

Her skin is still beautiful, soft brown and rosy. It is like very old deerskin gloves. When she was younger, she had silky chestnut hair, very European, but she let it go gray and then radiant moonwhite. She was long-legged and looked great in shorts and well-worn hiking boots. Our families went hiking together many weekends, on Mount Tamalpais, at Palomarin, on the Bear Valley Trail in Point Reyes. She was not patient with children who lagged behind on the path; she brought us sandwiches on black bread, and perforated raisin bars to eat by streams and rivers. My father, taking pity on us, brought Cokes and grape sodas and chubs of salami. She was an expert seamstress with great style and taste; she was also sort of cheap—she would say frugal—and bought impeccable accessories at Monkey Wards and Cost Plus.

She sewed some things for me over the years,

especially as I neared adolescence, so skinny that
nothing from the stores could do justice to my
peculiar beauty. She made me two tennis dresses
when I was twelve, sky-blue grosgrain trim on one,
embroidered cloth daisies on the other. My eighth-
grade graduation dress of periwinkle blue; a hippie
shift when I was fourteen, from a Cost Plus Indian
bedspread; a much bigger one when I suddenly
filled out and then some.

My mother and Gertrud raised their kids
together, played tennis at the club, fought for
left-wing causes, and shared a love of cooking
and reading, and both subscribed to *The Nation*
and *The New Yorker* for as long as I can remember.
Our families were at each other's houses all the
time. My father and Rex sailed on Rex's boats many
weekends, sometimes up the Delta for the whole
weekend. Gertrud was a server, manic and indus-
trious, my mother a mad little English archduchess
who had people wait on her. While Gertrud saved,
my mother charged; while Gertrud's marriage
lasted, my mother's ended when she was forty-
eight. She charged a fantastic new life for herself in
Hawaii, where she started a law firm. When she
moved back fifteen years later, she was broke, ill

with diabetes, and then early Alzheimer's. Gertrud
hovered over her, clucked, mended, tried as ever
to fix her.

After surviving breast cancer twice, Gertrud
was the one who got dealt the cards to be the sur-
vivor, the one who got to see how things came
out; one pays an exorbitant price for that honor. A
few years ago, my mother died, devastatingly. A
few years before that, Gertrud's husband died of
cancer, and twenty-five years ago, my father. These
were the people with whom she had planned to
grow old. She endured.

Our families are still close, and I am particularly devoted to Gertrud. This does not preclude
my shaking a fist at her in public or at meals when
she says aggressively stubborn things. "That's
enough out of you, old woman," I thunder, and she
shakes utensils in my direction, like a crab.

Until two years ago, Gertrud was still hiking
in the mountains, with me, with her friends, and
when you watched her, you could see how much
ground she had lost. Even as she had to steady
herself with a walking stick while she pointed out
alpine wildflowers—grousing that you should
know their names by now—you thought, Please let
me look like this at eighty. Then when you saw

her in the convalescent home after botched sur-
gery to replace her hip—frail, pale, defeated—you
thought, Please don't let me live this long. Please,
Jesus, shoot me. But then she resurrected one more
time, came home, set her life in order again. She
still lives alone, and drives; she keeps up her garden, with help, and makes people in our blended
family cheesecake for birthdays.

She looks iconic now, apple-doll-ish, small
as a child, terribly thin, still stylish and beautiful,
though. Stubborn as ever; impossible.

When her daughter called from Oregon last
week, and left me a message saying that Gertrud was depressed about selling her house, and
would I please give her a call, I got on the phone
immediately.

I hadn't even known she was definitely selling
the house. The last I'd heard, she was selling just a
parcel of land below the house her husband built.
This was where she had always wanted to die, in
this falling-down house where, from her deck, you
can see a broad swath of San Francisco Bay, Angel
Island, Alcatraz, the entire span of the Golden Gate
Bridge, the lights of San Francisco, the sailboats,
the ferries. We used to be able to see the railroad
yard from here, the trains, and walk a hundred

yards to the trestle that took you above the yard to Main Street, until it was all torn down.

For the last few years, she had spoken about how one day she might need to leave, for some sort of assisted-living apartment, but this was the first I'd heard of her actually doing so. We'd all been supportive of her keeping the house forever, but secretly hoped that she'd have a nice cerebral accident before she *had* to move, a nice sudden Hallmark death while dozing.

I called Gertrud and asked her what was happening. She was distraught. She was going up to San Rafael at five, to sign the papers selling both her house and the parcel of land. The man handling the transaction was one of Rex's old sailing buddies, and the prospective buyer was the grown son of childhood friends from Germany. "I can't talk to you or anyone now," she said.

"At least let me drive you tonight," I begged.

"No. I need to do this myself. Just pray for me." Now, this scared me badly, as she is a confirmed atheist. Her deep spirituality is absolutely anti-religious, entirely rooted in nature and in taking care of people. She has made her daily rounds all the years I've known her, taking food and comfort to sick friends. She was the local head of UNICEF forever.

Still, I have seen an amorphous interest on her face in the holiday prayers one of us always offers, when we lift up her husband, my father, my mother. I know she feels the three of them, then, in a way different from memory: more like when we light the paper that amaretti cookies come wrapped in, stamped with pale pink and blue and green, and make a wish as they flutter on fire up into the air, wisps of sparks and then ashes.

I told her I had to leave for an appointment in Berkeley but would call her from the car on my way back, to see if she'd changed her mind.

She can be so annoying and inconvenient, like most old people. Just that they've lived so long frustrates your hope of easy endings. They're going to die anyway—why are they clinging so hard to the life they had? I know the answer: It gives them happiness. All any of us has is this bit of time to-gether now. But the old, who can see so much and so little, hook into life with a lot of opinion and complaint, and this can be wearing. The only rea-son I do not feel like attacking her more often is that she isn't my real mother. But I've come close.

Every year when she goes with Sam and me to a writing conference in the mountains, there are times when I have to leave the living room of our condo to compose myself. We'll spend hours together happily, reading, making food for Sam and his friends, cleaning up after that; and I'll listen to her endless comments, opinions, grievances, and questions, and it doesn't bother me at all. I'll be an annoying old lady someday, too, with opinions on everything, if I live. Age itself is annoying, and weird. Everything gets solidified and liquefied at the same time. I honor her by simply noting the need for constant engagement. But then she'll criticize something, and in her honeyed, controlling voice I'll hear the burr of friendly fascism. It so pushes my buttons—speed dial. I'll hear coercion in her supposedly innocent suggestions, the hideous drive of the Viennese waltz—"You vill valtz!"—and the glittering pleasure of "I told you so." And let's not even get into the garbage eating.

Well, okay: but just briefly. Do all Europeans who survived World War II eat garbage? Not simply cutting off half-inches of mold on cheese to save the rest of it: I do that. I mean the insistence that the bit of toasted bagel that Sam left on his plate yesterday makes a perfectly nice breakfast today—for her. She's not trying to make me eat it, and still it enrages me.

"Gertrud!" I say. "That is garbage!"

Or I'll come upon her gnawing on an absolutely white cantaloupe rind that she's found on Sam's plate. Or she'll wrap up overcooked ravioli from yesterday that she wants to take with her when we leave tomorrow, to eat for dinner when I drop her off. It's table scrapings.

But mostly, we find enormous solace in each other. We read the papers together, angrily, muttering. She reads Noam Chomsky for pleasure. She brings me great chocolate.

We hike almost every day when we are in the mountains. On our last night together, two years ago, we went stargazing at High Camp, in Squaw Valley. Already at 7,500 feet, we took the gondola up to the meadow, where fifty others had gathered to watch a Perseid meteor shower. There were two astronomers to guide us, with powerful telescopes.

Gertrud was by far the oldest person there, by a good ten years or so. She was wearing a hat, warm clothes, and hiking boots, and she had her walking stick, ready for action. You could tilt your head back and see a shooting star every few minutes. Gertrud held on to my arm, leaned back unsteadily.

The astronomers started with easy stars, con-
stellations and planets, Cassiopeia and Venus, almost below the horizon; they showed us star
clusters, and told us how many millions of galaxies
there are, infinitely bigger than our old Milky Way,
trillions and gazillions of light-years distant, and
all the while there are shooting stars and showers
overhead. Gertrud leaned on me, held tight to my
arm, and whispered in my ear, "We don't need so
much information! Right there is the best thing of
all, our dear old friend the Big Dipper."

We had hiked on this exact spot of land the day
before, on our yearly wildflower walk, and the sky
then was as bright as the field of weedy yellow
flowers had been.

Gertrud won't wait in line. Maybe it is a European thing, like the garbage eating. Maybe she has
waited in enough lines to last a lifetime. But I took
my turn when she said she was steady enough to
stand alone. When I reported that you could see
twin stars and stellar graveyards through the telescope, she said rather huffily, "I'll just wait right
where I am, and see what I can see."

The stars were as close as berries on a bush.

After a while, though, Gertrud began to shiver.
The night was not that cold, but she is so thin. She

teetered as she held on to me, and I stood like a handrail while she got her balance. She held on so tight that it hurt: I could see that her knuckles were white, by the lights of the stars and the gondola. I rubbed her shoulders briskly, as you would warm a child just out of the ocean, and we headed back down the mountain.

I was reminded of that evening when I called her from Berkeley at three-thirty the day she was going to sell her house and asked her if she'd like me to pick her up. "Yes, please," she said. When I got to her house an hour later, she was waiting outside, ready for action again: this time, instead of hiking boots, she was wearing a dark blue knit cardigan with gold buttons, and a scarf tucked in around her neck; very nautical, still the admiral of her ship. She was teary but composed. All I knew to do was to be willing to feel really shitty with her.

"When did you decide to sell the house?" I asked when we started out.

She said with genuine confusion that she didn't know how it had come to be—she had meant to sell only the parcel. A number of friends had convinced her that it made sense to sell both properties now and rent the house back for a year. This would give her time to find a smaller place, with a garden and a view, and people around to help her in case she fell.

"Couldn't you hire someone to help around the house and drive?"

She said she had changed her mind too many times, had put everybody through too much already: the realtor, the buyer, and her children.

Everything in me wanted to save her—to offer her the extra room in our house, or promise to drop in on her every day. But instead I did an incredible thing, something I have not done nearly enough in my life: I did nothing. Or at any rate, I did not talk. Miserable, and desperate to flee or to fix her, I listened instead.

Fear and frustration poured out of her as we drove past my entire childhood, past the hillsides that used to be bare of everything, where we slid down the long grass on cardboard boxes, past the little white church on the hill, past the supermarket built on the swamps where we used to raft, past the stores on the Boardwalk, where the Christmas star shines every year.

Then, without particularly meaning to, just before we got on the clotted freeway, I pulled off the road and parked the car in a bus zone.

"Wait a minute, Gertrud. Let me ask you something: What do you want to do? What does your heart say?"

She answered after a long moment. "I don't want to sell my house."

"Are you sure?" This was shocking news, and the timing just terrible.

"Yes. But now I have to. I've changed my mind so often."

Neither of us spoke for a minute. "But that's the worst reason to do something," I finally said. She looked at me. "You have the right to change your mind again."

"Really, Annie?"

"Yep."

Gertrud glanced around with confusion, disbelief, misery. She dried her tears, reapplied lipstick, and picked at invisible lint on her blue knit sweater.

When we pulled onto the old friend's street, she said, "Oh, Annie. This will be such bad news for everyone else but me."

"There's a first time for everything," I said. "Besides, your friend's son can build a nice home for himself on the parcel."

Everyone was waiting for us when we arrived, and managed to be giddy and gentle at the same time. Gertrud was fussed over. These were not men in black capes with twirly moustaches, stealing her house away; they were dear friends. After a few minutes of small talk, she looked at the ground. Then she did not look up for a while. Everyone grew quiet, puzzled.

"I've changed my mind," she then said, firm, clear, deeply apologetic. "I don't want to sell my house. Only the parcel." I held my breath. Old age on a good day is a dance we don't know the steps to: we falter. We may not be going in the direction we'd anticipated, or have any clue at all about which way to turn next.

"Gertrud," they said, "are you sure?" She nodded and said, "Yes, yes," and held on to the arms of her walker so her knuckles turned white, as on the night of the meteor shower. Her voice was trembly. I remembered how she'd shivered from the cold. I remembered how the astronomer pointed out that the stars were not all one color: there are orange stars, red stars, pale yellow stars. Venus so close and bright I thought it was a plane, and through the telescope I could see fuzzy cotton balls hundreds of millions of miles away, stellar graveyards and stellar nurseries where stars were being hatched.

Barn Raising

On an otherwise ordinary night at the end of September, some friends came over to watch the lunar eclipse, friends whose two-year-old daughter, Olivia, had been diagnosed nine months earlier with cystic fibrosis. Their seven-year-old daughter, Ella, is Sam's oldest friend: they met in day care and have been playing together for so long that I think of her as Sam's fiancée. Now the family has been plunged into an alternate world, a world where everyone's kid has a life-threatening illness. I know that sometimes these friends feel that they have been expelled from the ordinary world they lived in before and that they are now citizens of the Land of the Fucked. They must live with the fact that their younger daughter has this disease that fills its victims' lungs with thick sludge, harboring infections. Two-week hospital stays for nonstop IV antibiotics are common. Adulthood is rare.

Twice a day, every day, her parents must pound her between the shoulder blades for forty-five minutes to dislodge the mucus from her lungs. It amazes me that Sara, the mother—fortyish, small-boned, highly accomplished—can still even dress herself, much less remain so tender and strong.

The night of the lunar eclipse, some of our neighbors were making little cameo appearances on our street, coming outside periodically to check on the moon's progress, as if it were a patient: "How's his condition now?" But Sara and I stayed outside and watched the whole time. It was so mysterious, the earth's shadow crossing over the moon, red and black and silvery, like a veil, and then receding, like the tide.

Ella calls her little sister Livia; she stayed overnight with us the day Olivia was born, and we cooked pancakes in the shape of the letter O to celebrate the baby's arrival. From the beginning, Olivia always got sicker than other babies; she caught colds that wouldn't leave, which led to coughs that sounded like those of an obese alcoholic smoker. But her doctor never found anything really wrong, and antibiotics always seemed to clear up the symptoms. Now she and I hang out together in her room and eat chocolate, and I tell her that in a very long time, when we both go to heaven, we should try to get chairs next to each other, close to the dessert table.

"Yes!" she agrees. She has round brown eyes and short yellow hair. What a dish! "More chocolate," she cries, and throws me the ball she is holding—I tell you, this girl's got game. I taught her to love chocolate, which her parents still hold against me.

Whenever I'm out of town I worry that there will be bad news when I come home, that friends will have come over to their house not knowing they were about to come down with a cold, and Olivia will end up back in the hospital on the two-week IV drip. She has a blue toy phone that she calls me on frequently. Sometimes when I am out of town, I imagine her calling me and chatting away on her phone. I was gone for a week of teaching at the end of summer this year, and I kept thinking of her. I almost called California to hear her voice. I was working too hard and staying up too late every night, and the people I was with were drinking a lot. I started to feel like a tired, wired little kid at a birthday party who has had way too much sugar, who is in all ways on overload, but still finds herself blindfolded and spun around for a game of pin-the-tail-on-the-donkey, and then pushed more or less in the direction of the wall with the donkey on it. But I was so turned around, so lost and overwhelmed and stressed, that I couldn't even find where the wall with the donkey was—or even in what direction it might be. I couldn't take one step forward without the chance that I was actually walking farther away from it. And it took me a while to remember that for me, the wall with the donkey on it is Jesus.

I didn't call Olivia, but I kept her in my prayers. I said to God, "Look, I'm sure you know what you're doing, but my patience is beginning to wear a little thin. . . ."

A few days before the eclipse, I arrived home but only after Sam had gone to bed. I lay down next to him and watched him sleep. There was an ordinary moon in the sky; I studied Sam by its light and felt entirely pointed in the right direction. Olivia's father, Adam, had left a message on our machine, letting us know that Olivia had been sick again while I was gone. They had managed to keep her out of the hospital, but it had been touch-and-go for days. Watching Sam sleep, I kept wondering, How could you possibly find the wall with the donkey on it when your child is catastrophically sick? I don't know. I looked up at God, and thinking about Olivia, about how badly scarred her lungs were already, I said, "What on earth are you thinking?"

The eclipse moved in such peculiar time. Maybe it's that I'm so used to blips and sound bites, instant deadlines, e-mail. But the shadow of the earth moved across the moon in celestial time, somehow slowly and fleetingly at the same astronomical moment. It seemed as if the moon were being consumed, and as if all the moons that ever had been were being consumed all at once. As if, in its last moments, you got to see the moon's whole life pass before your very eyes.

On New Year's Day, before her diagnosis, I was out at Stinson Beach with Sam and with Olivia and her family. They have a huge German shepherd, who is always with them; he hovers over Olivia, looking very German. He was with us on the beach that day, chasing sticks that Adam threw. It was one of those perfect Northern California days when dozens of children and dogs are running on the beach and pelicans are flying overhead, and the mountains and the green ridges rise behind you, and it's so golden and balmy that you inevitably commit great acts of hubris. Olivia seemed fine— happy, blonde, tireless. Just a few days before, her parents had taken her to the doctor for lab work, because of her severe colds. But she didn't have a cold on New Year's Day.

Then two days later Adam called with the news that she had cystic fibrosis. Now, seeing her the night of the eclipse, her upward gaze of pure child wonder, I find it hard to remember when she wasn't sick and harder to believe that she is.

Olivia laughs at all my jokes. The night of the eclipse I kept pointing to our dog, Sadie, and say- ing, with concern, "Isn't that the ugliest cat you've ever seen?" and Olivia would just lose her mind laughing.

After the diagnosis, we were almost too stunned to cry. Olivia's family has a tribe of good friends around them, and everyone wanted to help, but at first people didn't know what to do; they were immobilized by shock and sadness.

By mid-January, though, I had a vision of the disaster as a gigantic canvas on which an exqui- sitely beautiful picture had been painted. We all wanted to take up a corner or stand side by side and lift it together so that Olivia's parents didn't have to carry the whole thing themselves. But I saw that they did in fact have to carry almost the whole heartbreaking picture alone. Then the image of a canvas changed into one wall of a barn, and I saw that the people who loved them could build a marvelous barn of sorts around the family.

So we did. We raised a lot of money; catastrophes can be expensive. We showed up. We cleaned, we listened, some of us took care of the children, we walked their dog, and we cried and then made them laugh; we gave them privacy; then we showed up and listened and let them cry and cry and cry, and then took them for hikes. We took Ella and Olivia to the park. We took Sara to the movies. I took Adam out for dinner one night right after the diagnosis. He was a mess. The first time the waiter came over, he was wracked with sobs, and the second time the waiter came over, he was laughing hysterically.

"He's a little erratic, isn't he?" I said, smiling, to the waiter, and he nodded gravely.

We kept on cooking for them and walking the dog, taking the kids to the park, cleaning the kitchen, and letting Sara and Adam hate what was going on when they needed to. Sometimes we let them resist finding any meaning or solace in anything involving their daughter's diagnosis, and this was one of the hardest things to do—to stop trying to make things come out better than they were. We let Sara and Adam spew when they needed to; we offered the gift of no comfort when having no comfort was where they had landed. Then we shopped for groceries. One friend gave them weekly massages; everyone kept giving money. And that is how we built our Amish barn. Now things are sometimes pretty terrible for the family in many ways, but at the same time, they got a miracle. It wasn't the kind that comes in on a Macy's Thanksgiving Day float. And it wasn't the one they wanted, where God would reach down from the sky and touch their girl with a magic wand and restore her to perfect health. Maybe that will still happen—who knows? I wouldn't put anything past God, because He or She is one crafty mother. Yet they did get a miracle, one of those dusty little red-wagon miracles, and they understand this.

Sara was in a wonderful mood on the night of the eclipse. The viral cloud of autumn was about to descend, though, and this meant the family was about to find itself more exposed to danger, to cold germs, flu bugs, and well-meaning friends. There would be constant vigilance, fewer visits, endless hand-washing, extra requests for prayer. There are a number of churches in the Bay Area and in fact around the country whose congregations pray for Olivia every week. And maybe it is helping. Still, the specter of the cold season hung above Olivia's parents that night like the mysterious shape-shifting moon. Sam and Ella stood off by themselves like teenagers, Olivia hung out with her mother and me. We all stared up into the sky for a long time, as millions and millions of people everywhere were doing, so we got to feel united under the strange beams of light. You could tell you were in the presence of the extraordinary, peering up at the radiance beneath the veil of shadow, the intensity of that rim of light struggling through its own darkness. Olivia kept clapping her hands against the sides of her face in wonder, as if she were about to exclaim, *"Caramba!"* or "Oy!" When the moon was bright and gold again, she ran up the stairs to join her sister and Sam, who were cold and had gone inside to play.

Sara had very calmly watched her girls go, and I could see that these days, her daughters were the wall with the donkey on it. We stood outside for a while longer, talking about this last flare-up, how frightened Sara had felt, how tired. And I didn't know what to say at first. Except that we, their friends, all know that the rains and the wind will come, and they will be cold—oh God, will they be cold. But then we will come, too, I said; we will have been building this barn all along, and so there will always be shelter.

Falling Better

Last year, a few days after Easter, I was invited to Park City, Utah, to give some lectures, and had scammed a free ski week out of the deal. Sam had invited his friend Tony along, and I invited my friend Sue Schuler. She was a great companion, younger than I, but already wise, cheeky, gentle, blonde, jaundiced, emaciated, full of life, and dying of cancer.

She said yes. She had always loved to ski and was a graceful daredevil on the slopes. I started skiing only six years ago, and tend to have balance and steering issues. I fall fairly often, and can't get up, but I enjoy the part between the spills, humiliations, and abject despair—sort of like real life.

No one in her family, including Sue, was sure

whether she would able to ski, or if she would even make the trip at all. Except for me. No one could have known that she would die one month after my invitation. At any rate, I thought that if she saw those Wasatch Mountains, she'd at least want to try. I invited her because otherwise I was never going to see her again—she had cancer of the everything by then—and because she was distraught on Easter when I called to say hello. I felt she ought to have one last great Easter before she died. I felt that that would make up for a lot. Easter is so profound. Christmas was an afterthought in the early Church, the birth not observed for a couple hundred years. But no one could help noticing the resurrection: Rumi said that spring was Christ, "martyred plants rising up from their shrouds." Easter says that love is more powerful than death, bigger than the dark, bigger than cancer, bigger even than airport security lines.

Sue said yes, she'd meet me in Park City.

I'd only met her over the phone, through her sister, an old friend of mine. Barb was a kind of matchmaker, who recognized kindred souls in me and Sue, believers who loved to laugh. Barb had known me when I walked my friend Pammy through her last year of life. And call me crazy, but I did not immediately want to be friends with another dying blonde babe just then. However, I felt God's hand in this, or at any rate, God's fingers on the Rolodex, flipping through names to find a last-ditch funny left-wing Christian friend for Sue.

It was March of 2001. The wildflowers weren't in bloom yet; the bulbs hadn't opened. A month before she called me for the first time, Sue had been told that her liver and lungs had developed tumors. She had been in a deep depression for a while, but the reason she finally followed Barb's advice to call me was that various people at her church kept saying that she could be happy because she was going home to be with Jesus. This is the sort of thing that gives Christians a bad name. This, and the Inquisition. Sue wanted to open fire on them all. I think I encouraged this.

Also, some of her evangelical friends had insisted sorrowfully that her nieces wouldn't get into heaven, since they were Jewish, as was one of her sisters. So I said what I believe to be true—that there was not one chance in a million that the nieces wouldn't go to heaven, and if I was wrong, who would even want to go? I promised that if there was any problem, we'd refuse to go. We'd organize.

"What kind of shitty heaven would that be, anyway?" she asked over the phone.

That was the beginning of our friendship, which unfolded over a year and some change, a rich, condensed broth of affection and loyalty, because there was no time to lose. I couldn't believe how beautiful she was when we met: I hadn't expected that earthy, dark irreverence to belong to such a beauty. She started coming to my church soon after, and we talked on the phone every week. I had one skill to offer, which is that I would just listen. I did not try to convince her that she could mount one more offensive against the metastases. I could hear her, hear the fear, and also her spirit.

Sue called on New Year's Day of 2002 in tears, to say she knew she was dying.

I just listened for a long time; she went from crushed to defiant. "I have what *everyone* wants," she said. "But no one would be willing to pay."

"What do you have?"

"The two most important things. I got forced into loving myself. And I'm not afraid of dying anymore."

She got sicker and sicker. It was so unfair—I wanted to file a report with the Commission on Fairness, and I still want to ask God about this when we finally meet. That someone so lovely and smart and fabulous was going to die, and that horrible people I will not name were going to live forever—it broke your heart. At the same time, she had so much joy. She loved her family, her friends, and eating. She ate like a horse. I have never known a woman who could put it away like Sue. Her body was stick thin, and on top of it all, the skin on one leg was reptilian with the twenty-two skin grafts from her knee up past her hip—which she'd needed after contracting a flesh-eating disease at a hospital after one of her countless cancer surgeries.

I ask you.

This business of having been issued a body is deeply confusing—another thing I'd like to bring up with God. Bodies are so messy and disappointing. Every time I see the bumper sticker that says "We think we're humans having spiritual experiences, but we're really spirits having human experiences," I (a) think it's true and (b) want to ram the car.

Sue and I met one last time, on the Thursday

after Easter of 2002, in Park City, to celebrate the Easter holiday privately, a week late. We shared a king-size bed in the condominium. Sam and his friend Tony took the other room, reducing it to Pompeii within an hour. Then, their work completed, they shook us down for sushi money and headed out for the wild street life of Park City.

The thing about Easter is that Jesus comes back from the dead both resurrected and broken, with the wounds from the nails still visible. People needed to see that it really did happen, the brutality, the death. He came back with a body, not like Casper or Topper. He didn't come back as the vague idea of spirit returning. No, it was physical, a wounded body. He had lived, He had died, and then you could touch Him, and He could eat, and these four things are as bodily as life gets.

The first thing Sue and I did was locate a beautiful Easter Week service online, and we followed it to the book. Well—sort of to the book, in the reform sense of "followed" and "book." The first night we celebrated Maundy Thursday, commemorating when Jesus had Passover with his disciples before his arrest and gave them all communion. We used Coca-Colas for wine and Pepperidge

Farm Goldfish for the bread broken in remembrance of Him.

Then we washed each other's feet. Jesus had washed His disciples' feet, to show that peace was not about power; it was about love and gentleness, about being of service. Washing Sue's feet was incredibly scary. I did not feel like Jesus at first. I felt very nervous. I don't actually like to wash my own feet. But we put some soap in a Tupperware dish tub, and she sat on the couch, and I lifted her feet into the warm water and then washed them gently with a soapy washcloth. And then she washed mine.

I watched her sleep beside me in bed off and on all night. Sometimes she was so still that I was sure she was dead. She looked like a beautiful corpse, slightly yellow, slightly smelly, ethereal. And then she'd snore softly or open her eyes and look at me. "Hi, Annie," she'd say in a small voice.

In the morning after breakfast, the four of us took the ski lift to the summit. The boys disappeared. Sue was wearing a lavender ski jacket, and she weighed 110 pounds, on a five-foot-nine-inch frame, and she was wobbly and trembling. People turned to stare at her, because she was yellow and emaciated. She smiled; people smiled back. She had great teeth. "Oh yeah, and I used to be *built*," she said, as we got our bearings in the snow. "I used to have a *rack* on me." We stood together at the summit, staring at the mountain range and an endless blue sky, and then I suddenly fell over. She helped me up, and we laughed and then headed down the mountain.

Sue hadn't been on the slopes for years, and she moved gingerly at first; the air was thin and she had cancer in her lungs. Then she pushed down hard on her poles, and took off farther down the mountain. At some point she turned around and waited for me, and as soon as I saw her, I stopped and fell over. There I was, sprawled in the snow, with my skis at an angle over my head, like Gregor Samsa in "The Metamorphosis." She waited for me to get up and ski to where she stood, and then she taught me one of the most important things I'll ever learn—how to fall better. She pointed out that when I fell, I usually didn't fall that hard. "You're so afraid of falling that it's keeping you from skiing as well as you could. It's keeping you from having fun." So each time I fell, I lay there a minute, convinced I had broken my hip, and then she would show me how to get back up. Each time, I'd dust the snow off my butt, look over at her, and head down the mountain. Finally, after she saw that I could fall safely, she tore off down the slope.

We celebrated Good Friday that night. It's such a sad day, all loss and cruelty, and you have to go on faith that the light shines in the darkness, and nothing, not death, not disease, not even the government, can overcome it. I hate that you can't prove the beliefs of my faith. If I were God, I'd have the answers at the end of the workbook, so you could check to see if you're on the right track as you go along. But nooooooo. Darkness is our context, and Easter's context: without it, you couldn't see the light. Hope is not about proving anything. It's choosing to believe this one thing, that love is bigger than any grim bleak shit anyone can throw at us.

After the Good Friday service, Sue wanted to show me her legs, the effects of all the skin grafting. The skin was sort of shocking, wounded and alien as snakeskin.

"Wow," I said. She let me study her skin awhile. "I have trouble with my cellulite," I said, guiltily.

"Yeah," she answered, "but this is what me being alive looks like now."

She had fought so militantly for her body over

time, but she was also tender and maternal with it. She took long, hot baths at night, and then smoothed on lotions.

We slept well. The next morning we celebrated Holy Saturday, the day before Easter, when Jesus is dead and hidden away in the tomb, and nothing makes sense, and no one knows that He's going to be alive again. His disciples had left Golgotha even before He died—only a few women remained at the cross. So the disciples skulked off like dogs to the Upper Room, to wait, depressed and drunk—or at least, this is what I imagine. I certainly would have been, and I would have been thinking, "We are so fucked." Father Tom adds that there was a lot of cigarette smoke that night, and Monday-morning quarterbacking.

One thing Sue wanted to do before she died was to get a massage, to be touched sensuously again, so we decided to get massages on Holy Saturday.

"I'll tell you," she said, as we walked to the salon. "You don't see a lot of bodies like Sue Schuler's here in Park City, Utah."

She got a gorgeous male Indian masseur. He looked like Siddhartha. I got a tense white German woman. Sue and the Indian man walked off together, and she looked over her shoulder with such pleasure that they might have been going to their bridal suite.

My masseuse looked like she was impatient to start slapping me.

When I saw Sue again, an hour later, she smelled of aromatic lemon oil. I asked, "Did you feel shy at all?"

"Nah!" she said. "Not after I gave him a tour of the Bod."

Sue got up early on Sunday, the day we were leaving. The sun was pouring through the windows, the sky bright blue. She no longer looked jaundiced. She was light brown, and rosy. She made us her special apricot scones for breakfast. I tried to discourage her at first, because I didn't want her feelings to be hurt if the boys turned up their noses. "The boys won't eat apricot scones," I insisted. "They eat cereal, Pop-Tarts . . . traiiff!"

"Oh, the boys'll eat my scones," she said slyly. And they did. They ate all but four, which she packed up for us to take on the plane. Two actually made the drive to the airport in Salt Lake City. They were small, pale yellow, flecked with orange apricots, gone by the time we arrived home.

Ground

Voices

The good news is that we're all doomed, and you can give up any sense of control. Resistance is futile. Many things are going to get worse and weaker, especially democracy and the muscles in your upper arms. Most deteriorating conditions, though, will have to do with your family, the family in which you were raised and your current one. A number of the best people will have died, badly, while the worst thrive. The younger middle-aged people struggle with the same financial, substance, and marital crises that their parents did, and the older middle-aged people are, like me, no longer even late-middle-aged. We're early old age, with failing memories, hearing loss, and gum disease. And also, while I hate to sound pessimistic, there are also new, tiny, defenseless people who are probably doomed, too, to the mental ruin of ceaseless striving. What most of us live by and for is the love of family—blood family, where the damage occurred, and chosen, where a bunch of really nutty people fight back together. But both kinds of families can be as hard and hollow as bone, as mystical and common, as dead and alive, as promising and depleted. And by the same token, only redeeming familial love can save you from this crucible, along with nature and clean sheets.

A great friend who became a grandmother this week is already being tortured by the baby's parents and the grandbaby mama's family, and *the baby is five days old.* My friend wrote to say she was trying for compassion and focus on the big picture. I wrote back that these go only so far. What really helps is radical self-care, and revenge.

Okay, I was just kidding about the revenge. Sort of.

I *will* say that in the face of this, maybe patience is not an awful thing to practice. The alternative is to jack oneself up with passionate convictions, self-righteousness, wounded silence, and blackmail, like dear old Mom and Dad used to do. Hey, how did that go? Pretty well? Helping pump Dad out of his bizarreness, so there'd be Reaganomics trickle-down, and thus Mom would be semi-okay, and then maybe the kids?

The last time I had a chance to choose between the old ways and the new was a month ago, when various family members, me included, had fallen, each in separate areas, into hardships that simply couldn't all be happening at once but were—legal, mental, custody, spousal. And health. So we gathered around the dinner table at my house, to which we had brought roast chicken and heirloom tomatoes, cheese, brown rice, and buttery Brussels sprouts with lemon and soy, along with what everyone had secretly brought to the feast, the indigestible sorrows of life.

Over dinner, we threw everything old-school at our problems—intelligence and wit and compassionate listening, and also the unconscious effort to power up, by taking inventory of all the offending parties. We had a bright conversation, and lots of attack humor, everyone zinging like electrified molecules. And there I sat, cute wise Annie, being the butt of most of the comical attack humor, fending it all off while feeling more and more vulnerable and wishing they would leave.

That night, after everyone left, I cleaned up the kitchen, which is always my favorite part of any dinner party, even at my own house. Then, as I was walking toward my bedroom, past the riverbanks of my grandson's and niece's toys and art supplies, I heard a high-pitched, warped voice. It said, clear as a bell, "Annie." I stopped and looked around. Obviously I had imagined it. I did not hear it again and attributed it to a brain glitch. But when I got to my bedroom door, it called to me again, "Annie," like a sick, witchy, ancient woman. I went back to investigate. It was deeply weird, with no possible explanation, unless the dogs were punking me. Or, more likely, the cat. When I didn't see anything that could possibly explain it, I went to bed.

A few nights later, there it was again, without warning, and I wondered if I was losing my mind. Not, I might add, for the first time in my life.

It gave me the chill. It made me feel desperately alone. Like everyone, I've had a huge lifelong package of fear and self-doubt that was always waiting to claim me, which I've tried rather successfully to keep contained, but now there seemed to be a leak in the vessel. A friend once called this sense of being too alone "the desperate plain," the looming desolate stretch of ground, no trees to shelter you, no water, no way to escape, nowhere to hide or find comfort, strewn with rocks and a few random snake holes. You are stripped down existentially, you are naked, you are nuts.

The third time I heard the voice, I thought, "It's come for me." The "it" was the spooky internal voice made external, the black-dog voice of insomnia and hangovers. All the specters I've imagined and suppressed for fifty years were finally coming for me. I could hear this voice out loud, in my living room, wheedling: "Annie."

It was filled with supplication and despair, and taunting, like an earworm, the piece of music you get in your ear and try to shake, like a dog with a foxtail, but it won't let you go—it could be a jingle for a plumber or Metamucil. Only this one was the brainworm that has been there since I was a child, beneath all the activity, distractions, success and obsession and brilliant conversations and busyness and horns honking.

It is the voice containing the knowledge that my parents' lives were insane, and that caused me to be insane, too, and that will cause the little ones to be insane, too, someday.

The shrill, small voice used to say, "Tick tock, tick tock," but now it was saying, "We *told* you so. Crazy as a *looooon.*"

I did everything I could to keep the patient comfortable: I went for extra-long walks with the dogs, focused on my work, was extra-kind to myself. But I heard it again a few nights later.

I looked around in the general area it came from, where my grandson's toy box was, and I sorted through the toys carefully, shaking them to make them say my name.

None of the toys said my name. A good sign.

I looked through my darling niece's box of ersatz makeup. Maybe it was the blue glitter lipstick.

Above the toy box, to the right, were bookshelves. Was one of the *books* saying my name? I checked out this lead and came up empty. Excellent news. Next I tried to ignore it. I didn't want to have to call a psychiatrist or 911. I kept shaking it off, telling myself sternly that there would be an explanation, something ridiculous, worse than the books or the toys or the makeup wanting to say my name. Strangely, though, I who tell my friends everything didn't mention this one little sitch to anyone.

I hurried along to my bedroom each night. The prospect of hearing the voice was like a baited hook dangling right there, and if I bit, it would finally, after all these years, pull me into its huge whale self, swallow me whole. Poor old mind. It has been through so much, under extreme pressure from the day I was born, assailed by doubts, driven crazy by parents, by mean kids, bad skin, the losses of real life. And here I've climbed out, and usually feel good, competent, and generous, and then this hideous thing gets out of the coconut shell. "Annnie. Annnnnie."

It was like an auditory rash. It was Jiminy Cricket.

A couple of nights when it called me, I went purposefully to my bedroom, then tiptoed burlesquely back into the living room to outsmart it and catch it in the act. But it didn't speak to me those nights.

It has always drilled away at me, this diminishing, mocking voice—and I haven't even had bosses or husbands. I've mostly kept it buried or muffled, but there have been many times of frozen, shamed loneliness, in public, or with a sweetheart, or at family gatherings, or when deeply alone, like now.

One night after I tiptoed back to the living room, as I lay in bed with earplugs, I wondered if it might be something like those remote-control fart machines that people find so amusing: an old woman sits down at the head of the table at a restaurant for a birthday celebration, and the comical, desperate middle child pushes a button, and a loud splutter erupts.

But I looked and could not find a remote-control fart machine.

Prayer helped, prayer always helps, and mostly I had sweet, creative, spiritual days—mother, grandma, auntie, and sister days, in most ways the best of my life—and then every few nights it called to me. It was like I heard the owl call my name, with Bette Davis playing the role of the owl. I kept remembering Roman Polanski movies. The voice might as well have been saying, *"No good, no good, no good."* And, "What a stupid life you've had." I did not hear it on days when the family wars burned brightest. It haphazardly harangued and laughed at me, for trying to keep the world in order by poring over my ledgers, my possessions, obsessions, and achievements, while everyone else surely had a life of presence and fulfillment.

I'd hear it only at night, late, softly but clear.

But willingness comes from the pain, and when I got to the point of believing I had really lost my mind, another voice inside me stepped in, grown-up and gentle. This one said, "Well? Who knows. Maybe not . . ."

It was lovely and amazing. I was marshaling a parent whom I hadn't had consistently as a child, who assured me that we would figure it out, together. This person believed what I reported, and felt that my perceptions could be trusted or were at least worthy of investigation. My parents of origin more often explained how I must have gotten the wrong idea, because everything was actually just fine, couldn't be better.

And one night, this other presence suggested that since the demon with its hideous chipperness seemed to appear as I headed for sleep, we would stay up together until we found out what it was.

We sat on the floor with the lights on, the dogs beside me, and the kitty resting on the couch above us. I heard the silence of an ideal life, a beautiful creative home, now with a grandchild in it most days, pets, beloved friends, books. Of course, there was hugely screwed-up stuff going on in my family's life, too, that could not *possibly* be God's will for us, especially not for the young ones in my family. How can God possibly expect us to accept God's will, when it can be such awful stuff? Why would you possibly pray for the power to carry out God's will when, if God will just hear you out, you think it's a very poor plan?

And right that minute, I heard the small, shrill voice: "Annie, Annie." I moved on my butt toward the toy box and the bookshelves and sat in silence. I listened, like a scouting party for myself. Finally, I heard it again. I could tell that it wasn't coming from the toy box, but from the bookshelves. I sighed with relief and a sense of progress.

I scooched forward to some of my most beloved possessions, my books, which have been in almost the exact same place in the four years since I moved into this house. I sat and looked lightly upon them, practicing patience, until my eyes landed on a woodcut puzzle that I'd brought back from the Frankfurt airport the year before.

The puzzle consisted of five colorful jungle animals cut out from a board the size of a legal pad, with a tiny battery embedded in the back that gave voice to the animals: an ascending moan for the elephant, a strange *crick crick* for the crocodile, *eee eee eee* for the monkey, a mumbly roar for the

lion, and a *caw-caw* for the parrot. I reached for it.
All the parts were in place. I lifted the elephant
out, and when I replaced it, heard nothing. Same
with the lion, the monkey, the crocodile. But when
I lifted out the parrot and then fit it back into its
slot, I heard, "Annnnnnnie. Annnie."

I threw my head back, laughing—those fucking Germans!—until the kitty ran for the kitchen. I
followed after her, to get a replacement battery.
Talk about total overwriting by the universe. Here,
like everyone else I knew, I'd constructed my life to
keep the brainworm at bay, by often turning
everything on, all day and all night—the TV, the
computer, NPR, the car, the espresso maker, the
iPad, the crazy animated collage of life, the dis-
traction circus. Yet all the noises and voices and
feelings and memories that had somehow become
compressed in me, like oil from fossils, had been
rising from the earth into one soft cry, and it
was my own name. Me: Annie, beautiful, ruined,
touching, shadowy, loving, and mad-as-a-hatter
me. I put a new battery into the casing of the puzzle, replaced all the animals, and then lifted them
one by one: the elephant moaned, the monkey
squealed, the crocodile cricked, the lion roared,

and the parrot said, "Caw, caw." I patted my shoulder and laughed gently, and put the puzzle back on the lowest bookshelf. Then I got up to do the single most reliable, comforting, celebratory spiritual action I know: I put clean sheets on the bed and smoothed out their crisp freshness, soft as cool skin.

Ham of God

On my forty-ninth birthday, in April 2003, I decided that all of life was pointless, and I would eat myself to death. Three weeks earlier, George W. Bush had launched war on Iraq. These are desert days. However, after a second cup of coffee, I realized that I couldn't kill myself that morning—not because it was my birthday, but because I'd promised to get arrested the next day. I had been arrested three weeks earlier with an ecumenical bunch of religious peaceniks, people who still believe in Dr. King and Gandhi. Also, my back was out. I didn't want to die in crone mode. Plus, there was no food in the house. So I took a long, hot shower instead and began another day of being gloated to death.

Everyone I know has been devastated by Bush's presidency and, in particular, our country's heroic military activities overseas. I can usually manage a crabby hope that there is meaning in mess and pain, that more will be revealed, and that truth and beauty will somehow win out in the end. But I'd been struggling as my birthday approached. Bush had stolen so much from us, from our poor and elderly, since the very beginning of his reign, and especially since he went to war in Iraq. I wake up some mornings pinned to the bed by centrifugal sadness and frustration. A friend called to wish me Happy Birthday, and I remembered something she'd said many years ago, while reading a *Vanity Fair* article about Hitler's affair with his niece. "I have had it with Hitler," Peggy said vehemently, throwing the magazine to the floor. And I'd had it with Bush.

Hadn't the men in the White House ever heard of the word "karma"? They lied their way into taking our country to war, crossing another country's borders with ferocious military might, trying to impose our form of government on a sovereign nation without any international agreement or legal justification, and set about killing the desperately poor on behalf of the obscenely rich. Then we're instructed, like naughty teenagers, to refrain from saying that it is an immoral war that has set a disastrous precedent—because to do so is to offer aid and comfort to the enemy.

While I was thinking about all this, my Jesuit friend Tom called. Usually he calls to report on the latest rumors of my mental deterioration, drunkenness, or promiscuity, how sick it makes everyone to know that I am showing all my lady parts to the neighbors. But this time he called to wish me Happy Birthday.

"How are we going to get through this craziness?" I asked. There was silence for a moment.

"Left foot, right foot, left foot, breathe," he said.

Father Tom loves the desert. A number of my friends do. They love the skies that pull you into infinity, like the ocean. They love the silence, and how, if you listen long enough, the pulse of the desert begins to sound like the noise your finger makes when you run it around the rim of a crystal glass. They love the scary beauty—snakes, lizards, scorpions; kestrels and hawks. They love the mosaics of water-washed pebbles on the desert floor, small rocks that cast huge shadows, a shoot of vegetation here, a wildflower there.

I like the desert for short periods of time, from

inside a car, with the windows rolled up and the doors locked. I prefer beach resorts with room service. But liberals have been in the desert for several years now, and I'm worn-out. Some days I hardly know what to pray for. Peace? Well, whatever.

So the morning of my birthday, because I couldn't pray, I did what Matisse once said to do: "I don't know if I believe in God or not. . . . But the essential thing is to put oneself in a frame of mind which is close to that of prayer." I closed my eyes and got quiet. I tried to look like Mother Mary, with dreadlocks and a bad back.

But within seconds, I was frantic to turn on the TV. I was in withdrawal—I needed more scolding from Donald Rumsfeld, and more malignant celebration of what half the nation agreed, in April 2003, was a great victory for George W. Bush. So we couldn't find those stupid weapons of mass destruction—pick, pick, pick. I didn't turn on the TV. I kept my eyes closed and breathed. I started to feel crazy, and knew that all I needed was five minutes of CNN. I listened to the birds sing outside, and it was like Chinese water torture, which I am sure we don't say anymore. Then I remembered the weekend when eleven million people in the world marched for peace, how joyful it was to be part of the stirrings of a great movement. My pastor, Veronica, says that peace is joy at rest, and joy is peace on its feet, and I felt both that weekend.

I lay on the floor with my eyes closed for so long that my dog, Lily, came over and worriedly licked me back to life. That cheered me up. "What did you get me for my birthday?" I asked. She started to chew on my head. That helped. Maybe the old left is dead, but after we've rested awhile we can prepare for something new. I don't know who can lead us away from the craziness and barbarity; I'm very confused now. But I know that in the desert, you stay out of the blistering sun. You go out during the early morning and in the cool of the evening. You seek oasis, shade, safety, refreshment. There's every hue of green, and of gold. But I'm only pretending to think it's beautiful; I find it terribly scary. I walk on eggshells and hold my breath.

I called Tom back.

He listened quietly. I asked him for some good news.

He thought. "Well," he said finally. "My cactuses are blooming. Last week they were ugly and reptilian, and now they are bursting with red and pink blossoms. They don't bloom every year, so you have to love them while they're here."

"I hate cactuses," I said. "I want to know what to do. Where we even start."

"We start by being kind to ourselves. We breathe, we eat. We remember that God is present wherever people suffer. God's here with us when we're miserable, and God is there in Iraq. The suffering of innocent people draws God close to them. Kids hit by U.S. bombs are not abandoned by God."

"Well, it sure looks like they were," I said. "It sure looks that way to their parents."

"It also looked like Christ had been abandoned on the cross. It looked like a win for the Romans."

"How do we help? How do we not lose our minds?"

"You take care of the suffering."

"I can't get to Iraq."

"There are folks who are miserable here."

After we got off the phone, I ate a few birthday chocolates. Then I asked God to help me be helpful. It was the first time that day that I felt my prayers were sent and then received—like e-mail. I tried to cooperate with grace, which is to say, I did not turn on the TV. I asked God to help me again. The problem with God—or at any rate, one of the top five most annoying things about God—is that He or She rarely answers right away. It can take days, weeks. Some people seem to understand this—that life and change take time. Chou En-lai, when asked, "What do you think of the French Revolution?" paused for a minute—smoking incessantly—then replied, "Too soon to tell." I, on the other hand, am an instant-message type. It took decades for Bush to destroy the Iraqi army in three weeks.

But I prayed: Help me. And then I drove to the market in silence, to buy my birthday dinner.

I flirted with everyone in the store, especially the old people, and I lightened up. When the checker finished ringing up my items, she looked at my receipt and cried, "Hey! You've won a ham!"

I felt blindsided by the news. I had asked for help, not a ham. This was very disturbing. What on earth was I going to do with ten pounds of salty pink eraser? I rarely eat it. It makes you bloat.

"Wow," I said. The checker was so excited about giving it to me that I pretended I was, too.

How great!

A bagger was dispatched to the back of the

store to fetch my ham. I stood waiting anxiously. I wanted to go home, so I could start caring for suffering people or turn on CNN. I almost suggested that the checker award the ham to the next family who paid with food stamps. But for some reason, I waited. If God was giving me a ham, I'd be crazy not to receive it. Maybe it was the ham of God, who takes away the sins of the world.

I waited ten minutes for what I began to think of as "that fucking ham." Finally the bag boy handed me a parcel the size of a cat. I put it with feigned cheer into my grocery cart and walked to the car, trying to figure out who might need it. I thought about chucking the parcel out the window near a field. I was so distracted that I crashed my cart smack into a slow-moving car in the parking lot.

I started to apologize, when I noticed that the car was a rusty wreck, and that an old friend was at the wheel. We got sober together a long time ago, and each of us had a son at the same time. She has dark black skin and processed hair the color of cooled tar.

She opened her window. "Hey," I said. "How are you—it's my birthday!"

"Happy Birthday," she said, and started crying.

She looked drained and pinched, and after a moment, she pointed to her gas gauge. "I don't have money for gas or food. I've never asked for help from a friend since I got sober, but I'm asking you to help me."

"I've got money," I said.

"No, no, I just need gas," she said. "I've never asked someone for a handout."

"It's not a handout," I told her. "It's my birthday present." I thrust a bunch of money into her hand, everything I had. Then I reached into my shopping cart and held out the ham to her like a clown offering flowers. "Hey!" I said. "Do you and your kids like ham?"

"We love it," she said. "We love it for every meal."

She put it in the seat beside her, firmly, lovingly, as if she were about to strap it in. And she cried some more.

We kissed good-bye through her window. Walking back to my car, I thought about the seasonal showers in the desert, how potholes in the rocks fill up with rain. When you look afterward, there are already frogs in the water and brine shrimp reproducing, like commas doing the macarena, and it seems, but only seems, that you went from parched to overflow in the blink of an eye.

The Last Waltz

This is not a story about the best Christmas present I ever gave or received, but instead, it's a story about the best holiday present I ever saw, when, right before my cranky Scrooge eyes, I got to see light return to this dark world.

I've had a friend for more than twenty years whom I am very fond of, rather than close to. Her name is Carol Wagner, and she is in her mid-fifties. I first met her twenty-some years ago when she used to pick me up hitchhiking out in West Marin, where we lived. She had unruly curly hair and was a great reader and a down-to-earth modest proletarian type who worked at the post office in Stinson Beach. I was a little afraid of her at first because she was also on the school board, where she could be tough and crabby, but I always liked talking to her when she gave me rides. She was wry and smart and abided no bullshit, all of which I have always loved in a girl.

There is a beautiful plainness to her, a sense of someone who is solid and true, who has had a lot of losses in life and reasons to be bitter, but who isn't. A beauty of intelligence and soul shows in her face, the kind that pushes through and becomes visible when people have handled their stuff and their suffering with tenderness and courtesy. She has always had a gnarly, ironic personality, somehow both at a remove and in your face—she does not suffer fools—but she has also seen many people through their hardships over the years, and so she is loved and appreciated. People liked to see her at the post office when they picked up their mail, because she was just who she was. What you saw was what you got. And that is so rare, and so lovely, that it can be a little alchemical. The poet Molly Fisk once wrote in a poem about the post office: "When I open Box 592, there was Carol's curly hair and one third of her forehead, like an Advent calendar in springtime."

Several years ago, Carol got leukemia. She did

all the standard medical treatments, including enough chemotherapy to last a literal lifetime. She shook and she baked and she lost all those wayward curls, and she got very sick from the treatments. But they seemed to be working for a while, and the people of Stinson Beach, where she lived, cooked and shopped for her and drove her around and kept her company and donated buckets of blood. She sloughed off all the nonessential aspects of her life, tossed them out of the airplane so she could fly a little higher, but the cancer stripped her way down, as it does, and when the chemo was over, she built her life back up. Then there were a number of recurrences, and she needed more rounds of treatment, and life got stripped back to surviving the disease and the cure, and then she'd build her life and health back up all over again. You would think that God or life would hold everything else back, like a traffic cop holding back the traffic so the baby ducks can cross the street, but this was not the case. Real life reared its head: First, some of the people Carol loves most also got sick, and she did what had to be done to help them even as she tried to get well again herself. But as the psalmist tells us, joy comes in the morning, and it did. Carol's daughter gave birth to a big darling hunky chunky boy, and all that soft unarmored baby skin was very healing for Carol. But of course what the psalmist does not say is that at the end of the day, dusk will come again, too, and then night—and for a lot of us, this is the one real fly in the ointment.

When I saw her at a concert, she was doing whatever was essential and not too much else. She was living with the "What if?" that everyone shudders to consider and doing pretty well with it. You had the sense that she was still a pretty tough customer in her private life, though she was visibly softer. I think it was due partly to that luscious, succulent blue-eyed baby boy, of whom she spoke with great happiness, but it may also have been the fact that cancer can wedge a certain kind of person open, so that many new things can get in. My guess is that what got into Carol was the knowledge of how loved she is, and therefore, how safe, and you could feel that she was very thankful to have this knowledge, even at its exorbitant cost.

But then she wasn't okay again. The cancer came back, and eventually, as a last-ditch effort, the doctors gave her a bone marrow transplant. The people of Stinson Beach circled their wagons around her once more. Meals were prepared and delivered, rides were offered and more blood was given. Then tests determined that the transplant hadn't worked.

There was nothing left for the doctors to try, and everyone was very sad, especially Carol, who loves her daughter and that grand little grandson so much, but what are you going to do when there's nothing left for the doctors to do? If you're lucky, you get on with life. So when her friends started talking to her about the details of a memorial service, her main wish was to be there for it.

And she was. A few Saturdays ago she gave a party at the Stinson Beach Community Center. She wanted to say thank you to the people of her town for all they had done, to let them know that she had lived as long and as well as she had because of their friendship—all those meals they had cooked, all that blood they had donated, all those children they had babysat so their parents could cook or drive for her.

It was a party and also a service, because we had come with dedication, with loving intention and attention, which is what makes something sacred. The atmosphere was somehow both festive and sad, heartbreaking really, giddy, and warm.

The big barnlike community center usually feels huge and impersonal, with rather unpleasant lighting. It's not fluorescent but close, bright enough so you feel exposed rather than illuminated. This night, though, only a few house lights were on. There was a fire in the fireplace and Christmas lights on the tree in the corner and candles everywhere, and it made for wonderful soupy light that cloaked everyone gently. People brought Carol a whole living room, too, couches, throw rugs, easy chairs. Everything was so ethereal and familiar that it felt as if we were all moving through one another's dream. I spotted her right away in the center of all the people. (There must have been two or three hundred, instead of the fifty she expected.) She was wearing a purple velvet dress, and she looked wonderful. Her hair is shorter now, the grayish curls cropped close to her head, and she doesn't look like the same old person, because she isn't: hard has become soft, tough has grown more tender, and after all that chemo, all that dehydration, dry has grown lush again.

A bluegrass band was playing in one corner, and people were talking with a great liveliness, as if to say, "Right this minute, we understand that this is all there is, so let's really be together." People milled around at their shiny best, under the fairy lights, as if moving loosely through the big net that holds us all. Her friends had dressed up and brought food and left their bad stuff outside on the step with their umbrellas. They took that big barny space and made it feel so warm and intimate and lively that I kept thinking everyone was dancing. It was disconcerting, because the truth was, or at least the visible reality was, that besides a melancholy hula early in the evening, only a few people danced while I was there. But there was a kind of Rumi dancing under way: "Dance when you're broken open. Dance if you've torn the bandage off . . ." People danced unpartnered but not alone, as in certain square dances.

In all that warmth and soft light we were like flecks in olive oil, or dust motes in a beam of sun, swirling and dipping and lifting and distributing ourselves over that huge space, the particles becoming one community. How rarely do we get to float.

My friend Neshama and I hid over by the tables of food, waiting for our turn to see Carol. We ate everything that couldn't outrun us. Everyone eats so much at these events! Maybe it's because you have a body, and it's still here and wants your attention. Maybe you want a little extra weight so the wind won't blow you away. *Mangia!* There were dozens of dishes of food on the banquet tables, fancy and plain, hot and cold, meats and salads and desserts, but best of all were some tiny roasted potatoes in a huge covered dish, oily and crisp on the outside, tender on the inside, brownish red and striped with wilted rosemary. First they resisted, and then they utterly melted in your mouth.

I sidled up to Carol's daughter, who was holding that big baby boy. He is solid and jolly and mingly, and he threw himself into my arms without thinking, and I got to smell his clean baby soul and feel his wiggly toughness for a moment. Then he stopped, stared into my stranger's face, saw with horror that he had made a terrible error in judgment, and cried out for Security. His mother reached for him, smiling, and back in her arms, he smiled at me again; he actually all but winked.

I finally got to spend a few minutes with Carol. She looked happy in that warm light, with all her friends around. Some people seemed stricken, uncomfortable at having been invited to come say good-bye, as if this were very bad manners, or as though they had just found themselves on a ferry ride they'd never intended to take. But mostly people seemed to stretch enough to be able to open up to the fearful thought that Carol would probably

die pretty soon. In all of this shadow, she was glow-
ing, giving off softness. The baby kept looking at
her, flirting, and you could see how he kept hom-
ing in on her. And you knew watching her that
even though she did not want to be dying, she was
going to do so with the same elegant ordinariness
with which she has lived. She told me later, "I don't
hate dying of cancer—it's better than dying in
other ways, because it's giving me time."

"Time for what?"

"Time to repair, time to tell everyone how
much I love them." It is so lovely to celebrate the
life of a person who is still here, a chance to shine
our best light on her as she shone her light on us,
before the light goes out. "This purple is *not* going
to look so great on me when the jaundice sets in,"
Carol said, but in the meantime, in those moments,
she looked luminous, like she might just start
dancing momentarily. And she did. We hugged
good-bye, and I wandered off, feeling like Eeyore,
looking for Neshama, but I happened to turn back
one more time and saw Carol moving around on
the floor, dancing with her friend Richard to a
twangy and melancholy bluegrass song.

Pirates

Not everything is going to be okay. Trust me on this. Especially in late November. November has been the season of the witch—the time of darkness, rain, mold, and reckoning, as the end of the year approaches, and you subconsciously take stock in all that you did, or failed to do. This year, a month ago all the forces of darkness were unleashed. Two young friends were very ill. My dog was diagnosed with cancer. The details of a recent massacre in Syria came to light. Two people I love most in the world were in obscene legal marathons. One of them was in dire psychiatric shape. They left upset messages for me; their problems tore me apart, but there was not much I could do. I'm a recovering higher power: I deeply want to fix and rescue everyone, but can't.

I have to believe that a real higher power is struggling in this as much as we are. But horribly, if healing and care are going to get done, it will be love working through us. Us! In our current condition, not down the road, when we are in the fullness of our restoration, in wholeness, compassionate detachment, patient amusement. Us, now. It has taken years for me to get this well, which is to say, half as reactive and a third less obsessed with my own neurotic disappointing self. I don't agree with the pace of how slowly we evolve toward patience, wisdom, forgiveness. Anyone would understand if we gave up and settled, the way people settle for terrible marriages. But these are our lives. So we try, we do the work of becoming saner and more authentic, which is hard enough without truly monstrous people crashing our lives, often—not always—through marriage, although I am not going to name names. Well, maybe just one: Uton.

Uton is the most awful human in my family's life, the one whom, if I were not a Christian, I would call lying scum, except that I know that this person is precious to God. So let's say, then, a devious, two-faced lying child of God. And because for complicated reasons she can't sneer at us herself in public, she has two friends who serve as proxy sneerers. When we come upon her friends, they give us the stink-eye. It's sort of funny. Usually we just call one another to report an Utonic sighting, and laugh about it.

I went to the movies one Saturday to get away from it all, for solace, spur of the moment, with no makeup on, in my fattest pants. I hadn't eaten, as my favorite meal on earth is popcorn and a salted caramel chocolate bar, and I planned to treat myself. Sometimes, as is true for the Coneheads, only consuming mass quantities will do.

As I walked from my car to the theater, I saw two things. One, a long, long line, which made my heart sink. But at the end of the line was a tall man who looked just like my younger brother. And the man miraculously turned out to be my younger brother, with his wife. They were going to a movie I'd already seen. I fell in with them.

We hugged and kissed and compared notes on how excruciating the recent month had been for those we loved, and we also teased each other gently and laughed. Heaven. We slowly got nearer to the door. Then a voice rang out from behind us: "Hello, Anne Lamott."

I turned to see who it was, and saw Uton's best friend, way behind us. She is a buxom brassy blonde, with teeth like a pirate, named Tammy. She is the only sober alcoholic in our local community who makes my skin crawl. She called out, "Wow, everyone, it's authoress Anne Lamott!"

My brother put his hand on my shoulder and I took a deep breath. But I was not the only person who heard—a friend of Tammy's, many people ahead in line, heard and recognized her voice, too.

"Tammy," the man enthused. "Long time no see."

She called out his name and then came forward to hug him, ten feet ahead of us. I could see the cross she wears around her neck. She beamed at me. Then the friends she'd been in line with came up to hug him, too.

Then they all decided to stay there.

They were now many, many spots closer to the ticket counter.

I smiled, trying to shake it off and be a good sport. For people like me, the fight-or-flight instinct comes out in the desperate desire to fix, people-please, and create harmony. My rage usually goes underground and then pops up like a caterpillar, eating another leaf or bud in the garden or an oat bag of popcorn. Come to think of it, though, it's also sometimes expressed as a desire to stab people in the head or run them over. It is my deeply embedded limbic system, my shadow open-carry Tea Party person. I wouldn't be human without it, yet at a time like this, when an image flickered on my inside screen, of me tearing out a clump of Tammy's brassy blond hair—well, it more than gives a girl pause. It's the last frontier.

And things got worse. The people still behind us collectively decided there was now a forked line, two creeks merging into one stream of people passing through the doorway ahead.

I turned to the people now racing to be in Tammy's line and said, "There's just one line, folks," although clearly now there were two, the real line and the new rogue line.

I said to the second line, "Come on, you guys. It's really not fair. We've all been waiting." I threw my hands up good-naturedly. "Please get back in line."

But they *liked* their line. They weren't stupid.

Tammy, the leader of the rebel forces, now ahead of us, nearly to the doorway, opened her eyes wide and said, "Uh-oh, I think we're making Anne Lamott unhappy."

A lot of people laughed. I prayed, "Help me," and looked at the ground. Now the lines merged at the door, and people were taking polite turns: You go, I go. I was all but pawing at the ground, snorting through my bull nostrils.

My brother and sister-in-law were whispering encouragement, as if I were in labor.

My hands quivered. I put them in my fat-jeans pockets. I calmed myself the best way I could, asking my brother, "Did you by any chance bring a spear?" He frisked himself, shook his head apologetically. I asked my sister-in-law, "Do you have a flask of acid in your purse?" She rummaged around, produced and proffered two packets of moist towelettes, maybe hoping I could wash my hands of the whole matter. I accepted them. The world is so wrong, and it's a horrible feeling, like in the *Threepenny Opera* song, "The world is mean, and man uncouth." All I could do was hold my head high, wash my trembly hands, try to breathe. I know enough at sixty to believe whoever said never to fight with dragons—because to them, we are crunchy and delicious. So I washed my hands with one towelette, put the other in my pocket, smelled my lemony hands. Good smells bring such primitive comfort, and I somehow held my own, until more people moved to Tammy's line and I accidentally said, "It's not fair."

"No!" my son said later, mortified when I told him the story. "You didn't really."

Yes, I did.

Everyone in front of us turned to stare, as if I were wearing my Miles Standish costume.

Tammy stepped through the lobby door before wailing to her posse, " 'It's not fair.' "

Tears sprang to my eyes. My brother and his wife surrounded me, like white blood cells, and offered to drive me home. The crowd moved us through the door. Even when we got inside, a couple of people in the lobby turned around to see my weepy authoress self. It felt like so much of my childhood, those times when you felt like you were on a ferry dock and the boat with the happy people was pulling away, or as if Margaret Hamilton might come pedaling by. I was torn. I wanted to see the movie, feed myself the only way I can sometimes, by shoveling it in and down. But if I left, Tammy won.

On the rock face of loneliness, I laid my money down on the ticket counter.

I assured my brother and sister-in-law that I was okay, and sent them off to their theater. There were only five other people at mine, obviously a bunch of losers, none of whom was familiar. We sat as far away from one another as possible and gobbled our popcorn, like goats. I wondered why we were even at this unhappy indie movie. What do I have in common with police and gang members? "Shh shhh shhh," I soothed myself, and just watched. Then it came to me: I was asking the wrong question. The right one is: Where is God in gang warfare? And the answer is, The same place God is in Darfur, and in our alcoholism, and when children are bullied: being crucified.

I tried to concentrate on the movie but kept hearing Tammy mock me, and the laughter of the people in line. The memory was primitive, biblical—she was the serpent going, "Come on— this is an easier way to do it." It was her animal. We all grew out of gills, tails, and sharp teeth, but the animal we grew out of is still in there. It's usually layered over, inside the armature of civility, of being presentable. The animal can be "The Lottery," or it can be juicy, rich, with pure, raw life and a fierce vigor, so we aren't cut off from instinct. It can be dogs running, a monarch butterfly, a baobab, a whale. It can be Koko the gorilla, who told her teachers in sign language that she was a fine gorilla animal.

Something seized me and got in, what we religious types might dare to call holy spirit. One acronym for God that I like a lot is Gift of Desperation. Maybe, I thought, this one night I could try something new. Willingness to change, after all, comes only from pain. I'm not talking the big-T transformation—well, actually, maybe I am. I do crave radical change, but perhaps with a little warning—I'd prefer to be wearing some makeup, perhaps a hint of color. But two baby steps forward? I'll take it.

I decided in the darkness of the theater to shoot the moon, to find Tammy after the movie and say I was sorry. Who knows, maybe those two rogue leaders, Gandhi and Jesus, were right—a loving response changes the people who would beat the shit out of you, including yourself, of course. Their way, of the heart, makes everything bigger. Decency and goodness are subversively folded into the craziness, like caramel ribbons into ice cream. Otherwise, it's about me, and my bile ducts, and how unique I am and how I've suffered. And that is what hell is like. So whom was I going to echo, Gandhi and Jesus, or Tammy and me?

Look, can you give me a minute to decide?

Do you want to be happy, or do you want to be right? Hmm. Let me get back to you on this.

I sighed loudly and knew what I needed. It was not to army-crawl through the lobby of the theater or to think about all the ways in which Tammy needed to improve.

After the movie ended, I went to look for her, to apologize for my part in the craziness. I surrendered; I laid my weapon down. I got to have transformation, of the consignment-store variety, from the cringing exile, to the Beloved, to fine gorilla animal.

Did I find her? Of course not. Life is not the movies. It doesn't work out in a convenient and linear way very often. But I found me. I found my timeworn dignity. I found the second towelette in the pocket of my jeans and washed the salt off my fingers. Best of all, I found my phone in the car and called a friend. I had tears of laughter streaming down my face by the time I'd finished telling him the story.

As I drove home, I realized that Tammy was

probably telling the story to Uton now, comparing notes on my disgrace. But I shook my head. I had responded to myself like a friend. You can't get there from where I'd been, in line, to where I sat now. A few weeks later, I did find Tammy, in another line, at the market, although with three people between us. At first I thanked God that the view was blocked. Then I leaned to the side and poked my head out, so she could see me. She was holding a clear sack of apples and a tub of Cool Whip. I smiled and looked contrite, and then she smiled, too, a shy pirate smile.

Market Street

I woke up full of hate and fear the day of a peace march in San Francisco. This was disappointing, as I'd hoped to wake up feeling somewhere between Wavy Gravy and the sad elegance of Virginia Woolf. Instead, I was angry that our country's leaders had bullied and bought their way into preemptive war. Hitting first has always been the mark of evil. I don't think one great religious or spiritual thinker has ever said otherwise. Everyone, from almost every tradition, agrees on five things. Rule 1: We are all family. Rule 2: You reap exactly what you sow; that is, you cannot grow tulips from zucchini seeds. Rule 3: Try to breathe every few minutes or so. Rule 4: It helps beyond words to plant bulbs in the dark of winter. Rule 5: It is immoral to hit first.

I tried to pray my way out of the fear and hate, but my mind was once again a pinball machine of blame and ridiculousness. I had planted bulbs a few months before, but they had not bloomed yet, and I did not want to get out of bed. Like everyone I knew, I was despondent about the war. And I wondered if I actually even believed in God anymore. It seemed ridiculous, this conviction that I had an invisible partner in life, and that we were all part of a bigger, less punishing and isolated truth. I lay there gnashing my teeth, sure that what you see is what you get. This was it. This earth, this country, here, now, was all there was. This was where all life happened, the up and the down and the plus and the minus and the world of choices and consequences. Not an easy place, but a place full of significance.

I clutched my cat as I used to when my parents fought, a life preserver in cold, deep water.

But then—a small miracle—I started to believe in George W. Bush. I really did. In my terror, I wondered whether maybe he was smarter than we thought he was, and had grasped classified intelligence and nuance in a way that was well above my own understanding or that of our era's most brilliant thinkers.

Then I thought: Wait—*George Bush?* And relief washed over me like gentle surf, because believing in George Bush was so ludicrous that believing in God seems almost rational.

I decided to start from scratch, with a simple prayer: "Hi!" I said.

Someone or something hears. I don't know much about its nature, only that when I cry out, it hears me and moves closer to me, and I don't feel so alone. I feel better. And I felt better that morning, starting over. No shame in that—Saint Augustine said that you have to start your relationship with God all over from the beginning, every day. Yesterday's faith does not wait for you like a dog with your slippers and the morning paper in its mouth. You seek it, and in seeking it, you find it. During the Renaissance, Fra Giovanni Giocondo wrote:

No heaven can come to us unless our hearts find rest in it today. Take heaven!

No peace lies in the future which is not hidden in this present little instant. Take peace!

And so I roused myself and went to meet some friends in San Francisco.

We milled around the Embarcadero, where you could see endless sky and bay and a Möbius strip of the '60s, a massive crowd gathered once again on sacred ground. Haranguers harangued us from various sound systems unimproved in the past thirty-five years, like heavy metal played backward at the wrong speed. But the energy and signs and faces of the crowd were an intoxicating balm, and by some marvelous yogic stretch, we all stopped trying to figure out whom and what we agreed with, and who the bad elements were: The socialist haranguers? The Punx for Peace, who had come prepared with backpacks full of rocks? The Israel haters? The right-wing Zionists? You just had to let go, because Market Street was wide enough for us all, and we began to march, each a small part of one big body, fascinatingly out of control, like protoplasm bobbing along.

The sea of people looked like a great heartbroken circus, wild living art, motley and stylish, old and young, lots of Buddhists, people from unions and churches and temples, punks and rabbis and aging hippies and nuns and veterans—God, I love the Democratic Party—strewn together on the asphalt lawn of Market Street. We took small shuffle steps, like Zen monks in a crowded wedding procession. It was like being on a conveyor belt, overwhelming and scary, because you might trip and get stepped on, but once you were really on the street, you could sit by the curb and sob, or adjust to it. It's disturbing to not walk with your usual gait, to move at once so slowly and with such purpose. I felt I was trying to pat my head and rub my stomach at the same time.

The "I" turned into "we." You shuffled along with your friends, moving at the pace of the whole organization, moving to the heartbeat of the percussion. You saw people you knew, and hung out awhile, and then they moved away, and new people fell in step beside you and offered you comments and gum. Whoever came along came along. The goodwill gave you a feeling of safety in this mob, a fizzy euphoria despite the grim reality of these times. Songs I've loved for decades were sung— "We Shall Not Be Moved," "Down by the Riverside," "Give Peace a Chance"—and then we'd tromp along, and the peace-march wave rose again, a joyful roar of solidarity rippling out from the front, over us, then picked up by those behind.

There was gaping, and a lot of volition; you were swept along, but the crowd had a self-correcting mechanism—it kept letting go of what wasn't quite right, the more raw, angry elements, the strident and divisive. It was a Golden Rule parade: you acted the way you wish the government would act, with goodness and tender respect, and this held the peace. The splinter groups that went crazy later and trashed everything were peaceful when they were with us. I saw only friendliness, sorrow, goodness, and great theater. My favorites were the people dressed as sheep on stilts, who resembled huge silver masked-ball aliens, with horns and curly tinsel wool, like puppets that Louis XIV might have commissioned. No one had any idea why they were sheep, or why they were on stilts. Maybe they were peace sheep, and maybe they just wanted to see better.

The Mothers in Black moved solemnly in the middle of the throng, steadfast and profound, witnessing for peace. They dressed in black, like the Madres in South America. They stopped you with their presence, like punctuation, made you remember why you were here.

Two things carried the day: regular people saying no to power, and glorious camaraderie. We were sad and afraid, but we had done the most radical thing of all—we had shown up, not knowing what else to do, and without much hope. This was like going on a huge picnic at the edge of the fog, hoping you would walk through to something warmer. The mantra you could hear in our voices and our footsteps was "I have a good feeling!" The undermutter was silent, spoken with a sort of Jewish shrug: "What good will it do to do nothing?"

The barricades were broken down for once, between races, colors, ages, sexes, classes, nations. There are so few opportunities for this to happen; at first, it feels like us versus them, and then you're shoulder to shoulder with tens of thousands of people, reading one another's signs, signs that pierce you or make you laugh out loud. You rub shoulders, smell the bodies and the babies, and pot and urine and incense and fear, and everyone's streaming past, including you. For once, you're part of the stream, and in that, in being part of it, you smell the pungent green shoots of hope. The feeling may be only for the moment. But it's a quantum moment: it might happen again, and spread and spread and spread; and for a moment and then another, there's no judgment, no figuring out, just an ebullient trudge, step, step, step.

People sang, and babies cried, and your feet started to hurt, and you wanted to go home, and just then the broad-bottomed Palestinian women started chanting, "This is what democracy looks like. This is what democracy looks like."

Wow. That's the prayer I said the morning after the peace march: Wow. I felt buoyed by all those people walking slowly together down Market Street, by the memory of the peacenik dogs with kerchiefs around their necks, the Mothers in Black, and the peace sheep. Then, amazingly, only a few days later, the very first bulbs began to bloom. Within a week, there were dozens of daffodils in the yard. When this finally happens in late winter every year, I'm astonished. I've always given up. In November and December when I plant them, I get swept up in the fantasy that the earth, after so much rain, will be rich and loamy. Planting bulbs sounds like a romantic and fun thing to do, but it never is. The earth is rocky and full of roots; it's clay, and it seems doomed and polluted, yet you dig holes for the ugly, shriveled bulbs, throw in a handful of poppy seeds, and cover everything over, and you know you'll never see them again—it's death and clay and shrivel. Your hands are nicked from the rocks, your nails are black with soil. December and January have been so grim the past few years, and this year the power kept going out, and everyone was crazy as a rat. Yet here we are in February, with war drums and daffodils every-where, and poppies waiting in the wings.

ACKNOWLEDGMENTS

Thank you, Jake Morrissey and Geoff Kloske, supreme commanders of Riverhead Books and of my life. Thank you, Anna Jardine, for brilliant and exasperating copyedits all these years. You have saved me from looking illiterate more times than I can count. Thank you, Alexandra Cardia and Katie Freeman and Lydia Hirt, and all the other rascally Riverhead rabbits.

Thank you, Sarah Chalfant, my gorgeous agent and friend.

Thank you, Steven Barclay and Kathryn Barcos and all the peeps at the Barclay Agency.

Clara Lamott, you are our sunshine, as Sam often says.

All writers are doomed without great writing friends to keep them honest, push them to make the work better, encourage and nag, celebrate or commiserate. Thank you, Doug Foster, Mark Childress, Neshama Franklin, Janine Reid.

And most of all, to St. Andrew Presbyterian Church, Marin City, California, and Pastor Veronica Goines. Services at eleven.